don't ignore MY MIND

don't ignore MY MIND

The Story of Robert Kaplowitz

ROBERT KAPLOWITZ

with Isabel Hogue, revised by Lucas Weeks

authorHOUSE®

AuthorHouse™
1663 Liberty Drive
Bloomington, IN 47403
www.authorhouse.com
Phone: 1-800-839-8640

Published by AuthorHouse   04/16/2013

ISBN: 978-1-4817-3571-1 (sc)
ISBN: 978-1-4817-3575-9 (e)

Library of Congress Control Number: 2013906409

Any people depicted in stock imagery provided by Thinkstock are models, and such images are being used for illustrative purposes only.
Certain stock imagery © Thinkstock.

This book is printed on acid-free paper.

Because of the dynamic nature of the Internet, any web addresses or links contained in this book may have changed since publication and may no longer be valid. The views expressed in this work are solely those of the author and do not necessarily reflect the views of the publisher, and the publisher hereby disclaims any responsibility for them.

"Doctor, are you telling us our son has no potential of any kind?" Bob's father demanded. "That we should leave him somewhere to sit and rot?"

"Well, truthfully, I don't see any other possibility."

Bob's parents knew the doctor was wrong. They knew there had to be other possibilities. But it took years of searching, frustration, and failure before they—and Bob—discovered what they were.

To Jack Kaplowitz (1914-2012)
Gerald and Nancy Korde and Family
Ruth Provisor Kaplowitz (1917-1959)
Charlotte Brawer-Kaplowitz (1916-2007)
Joyce Grant Kaplowitz
Irvene Brawer
and
Barney Brawer

Odd
this twisted form
should be
the work of
God.
God
Who makes,
without mistakes,
the happy norm,
the status quo,
the usual,
made me,
you know.
The Royal Palm
He made;
and, too,
the stunted pine.
With joy
I see the lovely shapes.
With pride
I live in mine.
*   *   *

No accident I am:
a Master Craftsman's
plan.

—Ruth Bell Graham

Contents

Foreword

The light of nature shows there is a God Who has lordship and sovereignty over all; is good, and does good to all; and is therefore to be feared, loved, praised, called upon, trusted in, and served with all the heart, and with all the soul, and with all the might. (Westminster Confession of Faith)

The goodness of God is obvious to anyone who takes a walk in the woods. Rabbits hop, birds sing, the Redbuds blossom, and rain falls on the just and the unjust. If the walk continues into evening, the starry host declares His glory. Yet there are parts of nature that don't seem to point so directly to our Creator's goodness. Lord Tennyson is right to take a jab at our facile talk of God's goodness and love:

Who trusted God was love indeed
  And love Creation's final law —
  Tho' Nature, red in tooth and claw
With ravine, shriek'd against his creed — 1[1]

If nature shrieks against the Christian creed that God is love, Bob Kaplowitz has always heard that shriek. Talk of God's love and goodness has never been cheap for him.

Since birth, Bob's body has been wracked by Cerebral Palsy, so he's spent his life utterly dependent on others. Halfway through the night, one of his Bobbites[2] is wakened by an alarm clock, gets up, goes into Bob's room, and rolls

---

[1] Alfred, Lord Tennyson; *In Memoriam*
[2] "Bobbite" is the affectionate name given the men who live with Bob and care for him.

him over so he's more comfortable and doesn't get bedsores. Then, in the morning, another Bobbite rolls Bob out of bed, brushes his teeth, dresses him, lifts him into his wheel chair, pushes him into the dining room, feeds him, holds a straw in his mouth so he can drink . . . and the day goes on like this until it's time to lift Bob back onto his bed for the night.

Maybe the hardest part of Bob's life is the difficulty he has making himself understood. A New York Jew by birth, Bob has a dry, self-deprecating (and therefore delightful) sense of humor. Repartee comes to him as easily as swimming to a fish. But jokes or insults bouncing around our minds remain far from the minds of our friends and loved ones; they have to be formed, spoken, heard, and understood before the laughter comes and we're made merry. Those who move past affection for Bob, to love, often find themselves wishing they knew what he was thinking. Right now—not three minutes later after we've finished asking him to repeat himself three or four times and finally been able to make sense of his wheezes, hisses, and pops. If we find the delay frustrating, it's not hard to imagine how wearisome Bob finds it.

So for Bob, the Fall—when Adam took and ate the fruit God had forbidden him—is no Jewish myth or finer point of Christian theology. It's the center of his existence. Every minute of every day, he's faced with the Fall's consequences in his own body. His brokenness and dependency remind him of man's need of a remedy for Adam's sin. So when he reads the Old Testament prophet, Isaiah, Bob is comforted to see that the Messiah shares our shame and suffering, but that being God's perfect Lamb, His suffering is redemptive:

> *He is despised and rejected of men; a man of sorrows, and acquainted with grief: and we hid as it were our faces from him; he was despised, and we esteemed him not. Surely he hath borne our griefs, and carried our sorrows: yet we did esteem him stricken, smitten of God, and afflicted. But he was wounded for our transgressions, he was bruised for*

our iniquities: the chastisement of our peace was
upon him; and with his stripes we are healed. All we
like sheep have gone astray; we have turned every
one to his own way; and the LORD hath laid on him
the iniquity of us all. (Isaiah 53:3-6)

Believing in the Messiah, Bob faces his suffering through faith—faith in the goodness and love of our Creator Who sent His Only Begotten Son into this world to give His life a ransom for all, the Lamb of God Who takes away the sin of the world.

Yes, there is suffering in this world, but God is good. He doesn't watch from afar, a cruel tyrant entertaining Himself with our agony. Rather, He Himself bears our griefs and carries our sorrows. The chastisement required for our peace is upon Him and by His stripes we are healed.

Put it all together and it becomes clear why Bob is a treasure within our church family. His suffering is chronic but He hasn't become depressed. We often fail him but Bob's no cynic. He's humiliated all the time—I've even seen him dropped on the concrete in front of my house—but Bob is neither punitive nor proud. He's never been able to marry, but each young man who lives in his house and gets engaged is proud to ask Bob to be his best man, and Bob obliges with dignity and joy. We've had lots of parties at Bob's house, but no pity parties. Instead, there's good meat and fine wine garnished with laughter, arguments, and insults galore.

Why such cheer?

Because Bob doesn't blush to say that the God of Scripture is absolutely sovereign over all His Creation and that He does all things well. That our suffering is a treasure in His hand, bringing only good to those who love God and are called according to His purpose.

Speaking personally, I find Bob delightful. Each year he gives me a calendar illustrated with pictures of jackasses, so it's clear he has a certain affection for me, also. Beyond the personal, though, I thank God for allowing our church to have Bob and his Bobbites in our midst. Many of our young men have lived with Bob, learning leadership through humble service. So many, in fact, that we've taken to referring to Bob's house as "our finishing school for young men."

So now, you have Bob's book and you're about to read what he has to say for himself. Let me say, you have it easy! You'll understand everything he says the first time, and perfectly. But Bob has it easy, too, because he won't have to repeat himself. He's already done that with Isabel Hogue and Lucas Weeks, so the hard work is done and you're the beneficiary.

Then again, maybe you won't understand Bob after all? Without faith in Jesus Christ, little of this book (and increasingly less of it as you move toward the end) will make sense. But if you love God with all your heart and soul and mind and strength, you'll find that your own experience and faith aren't really that different from Bob's. And with Bob, you too will confess there is a God Who has lordship and sovereignty over all; is good, and does good to all; and is therefore to be feared, loved, praised, called upon, trusted in, and served.

Tim Bayly
April 26, 2008

CHAPTER 1

My Childhood

I'm sure it was my father's resolve and sense of humor that pulled our family through my difficult early years. My dad, Jack Kaplowitz, was the youngest of four children born to a family of Polish immigrants. Although the family culture was Jewish, my paternal grandmother is the only relative I can recall who actually went to temple.

During the years before World War II, Dad studied architecture at Cooper Union in New York. There wasn't a big demand for architects during those depression years, and Dad saw that he would make a poor living, if any. Characteristically, he was undaunted by the setback and decided instead to go into business. He was occupied one day at one of his early enterprises, a sporting goods shop, when the young woman who was to become his wife and my mother came in to buy a sweater. Her name was Ruth Provisor and Dad's family loved her from the beginning. Dad, nonetheless, kept the matchmakers in the family in torment, never letting them know for certain which way the romance was heading. His teasing only added to the excitement that builds before a Jewish wedding.

I was born into the world on May 8, 1948. Not many days after my arrival, my parents noticed that my arms and legs jerked and trembled sometimes. It happened often enough that before I was eight weeks of age, my parents became convinced that something was wrong. None of the doctors who examined me could explain it to their satisfaction. One doctor told them it was a behavior I'd outgrow (fortunately for me, my parents didn't believe him).

Finally, they found a doctor who made sense. I had cerebral palsy. Cerebral palsy is a birth-related problem that is more common than most people realize. In one form or another, it appears more frequently than Down's syndrome. Mother and Dad had never heard of it, but they learned that my jerking and trembling were evidence of brain damage. The doctor then explained that the damage had occurred either before or during birth. It was not possible to say when or exactly how it had happened. Besides, now that the damage was done, it didn't matter.

The doctor was frank with my parents and could offer little hope for my future. As I grew older, any combination of developmental disabilities would become evident: learning problems, speech impairment, involuntary movements, and probably mental retardation. He could promise only one thing. I would not outgrow cerebral palsy — ever.

As a little boy, it didn't bother me that I had cerebral palsy. I did notice, however, that I could not do everything that the other boys could do. I noticed that I was the only one who depended on someone else to take me to the bathroom.

Gerald, my only sibling, was five years old when I was born. We spent our boyhood years in a quiet, Jewish neighborhood in Passaic, New Jersey, part of the vast New York metropolitan area. Dad's was the dominant personality in the family, but most of my early memories revolve around Mother, music, and school.

~

My mother was neither a musician nor a singer, but had been raised in a Jewish household where everyone listened to classical music and opera. She adored music, especially opera. She listened to music on the radio quite a bit, but one of her joys in life was her small collection of recordings. Mother loved to shop in New York City and occasionally found her way into a record shop. It wasn't until she joined a mail-order record club, however, that her collection really expanded. During my childhood years, she and I spent hours on the couch in our den, snuggled up together, listening to opera on those wonderful 33 1/3 rpm long play records.

Somehow, Mother sensed that I had an intelligent and hungry mind. During our times of listening to music together, she told me the story of each opera, explaining the action to me while the record played. At a very young age I could identify the music of: Puccini's *Madama Butterfly*, *La Boheme*, and *Tosca*; Mozart's *The Marriage of Figaro*; Rossini's *The Barber of Seville*; Strauss' *Die Fledermaus*; Verdi's *Rigoletto* and *La Traviata*; and Bizet's *Carmen*. I was probably four years old the first time Mother played Carmen for me. The overture, of course, came first. From the moment the first notes of the stirring march reached my ears, I was caught up in the flow of sound. I inwardly gamboled to the joyful music until, without warning, it became sinister and slow. The sudden change frightened me so that I cried. Mother sensed then that my emotional response to music was very keen and she skipped the overture whenever she played Carmen after that. Another fright came over me when I first heard a recording of Caruso, the great tenor. In this case, however, my tears were more understandable. The old 78-rpm recording Mother owned was horribly scratched.

Besides opera, mother played music by Beethoven, Brahms, Grieg, Liszt, Tchaikovsky and Rachmaninoff. She would teach me something about each orchestra, conductor, composer, and composition.

She also loved musical shows and dance music. In my mind's eye, I can still see Mother dancing a rumba or cha-cha while straightening up the house. Actually, I think she just wanted an excuse to dance. Mother disliked doing housework and delegated most of it to Anna, our housekeeper. As housekeepers go, however, Anna was of the same temperament as Mother. The two women were satisfied if the house only looked clean. Our kitchen might appear to be spotless, but one peek in a drawer brought out the truth. I don't know how bad it got, but more than once Mother's sister Eleanor came to our house with the express purpose of straightening up our drawers, cabinets, and closets. This isn't as dramatic as it may sound. Intervening is one of the dominant Jewish female attributes and it meant that Aunt Eleanor cared about us. Mother also exhibited it, though to a lesser degree. One evening, she and Dad were dinner guests at the home of a friend. Mother took one look at the silverware laid on the table and said, "My God, this stuff is filthy!" I don't know how that remark changed the tone of the evening, but knowing that Mother was generally considerate of other people's feelings, I'm sure the silverware really must have been dirty or she would not have said so.

Beyond her role as housekeeper, however, Anna was an important part of our household. Having the freedom to leave me alone with Anna at times was a necessary relief for Mother. Even with Dad's help, caring for me day in and day out exhausted her energy. By the time I entered school at four years of age, I still required constant attention. Although I couldn't speak coherently, I babbled constantly. I either crawled or was carried, and Mother still had to feed me, clean up after me, and change my diapers.

~

My formal education began at the Cerebral Palsy Center in Clifton, New Jersey. The Center was just ten blocks from our home in Passaic and I rode to school in a taxi that the public school district provided. I remember that when I was very small, after stopping at the school entrance the taxi driver would lift me out of the cab and hand me over to someone who then carried me into the one-story, red brick school building. The classes at the Cerebral Palsy Center were organized like those in a one-room school. The younger children were in either the kindergarten or the primary grade classroom and the older ones were in a classroom called the multiple grade. At age nine, I was promoted to the multiple grade. In all three classes, the students were a mix of slow learners, mentally retarded children, and children of normal intelligence. Assignments were given to each student individually.

Scholarship is prized in Jewish families, so it was natural for my parents to insist that Gerald and I do well academically. No one in my family treated me as if I was mentally retarded or expected less of me because I went to school with mentally disadvantaged children. My brother and I were made to feel guilty if we didn't do our best work. Every day Mother made sure Gerald did his homework, and while she prepared dinner, listened to me describe what I had studied in school that day. It was a great comfort to me, coming home from school to Mother, who knew me and understood me. During our talks before dinner, I sometimes made remarks about how stupid I thought some of my classmates were. Mother allowed me to privately express my frustration with my classmates, but cautioned me to always treat them kindly. She often reminded me how fortunate I was to have a good mind.

Looking back over my childhood, I feel fortunate to have been born during the years following World War II, a time when the study of handicapped children and programs for them were expanding rapidly. One shortcoming of the research, however, was that the experts often focused more attention on the handicap itself than on helping the handicapped child live a meaningful life. I think the Cerebral Palsy Center was typical of schools for the handicapped during the 1950s. The emphasis of their program was on occupational and physical therapy. This meant that the students spent a great deal of time learning functional skills and improving whatever physical abilities each child might have. Formal education was a secondary concern.

Though the therapy experts of that day were moving in the right direction, many of their expectations for the handicapped were not realistic. For example, considerable time was spent teaching me to walk with a cane. I could hardly stand upright, and even with short braces on my legs, every step was labor. Despite years of training, by the time I turned fourteen my size and poor balance made the exertions they called "walking" impossible. I've been in a wheelchair ever since. I also worked hard at learning to dress myself. The effort was totally impractical because it took me the whole morning just to pull clothes on. And even then I needed help with the finishing touches. My stiff fingers couldn't subjugate buttons, zippers, or shoelaces. The reality I came to accept was that for the rest of my life, someone would have to assist me with every physical task.

In spite of the impracticality of some of my training, my time in therapy was not wasted because I learned larger lessons. For instance, learning to place a forkful of food into my own mouth gave me brief satisfaction. Learning to persist with an effort, even when my arms refused to obey my brain, had a lasting effect on my attitude and self-image. Mother understood my frustration and always encouraged my efforts by saying things like, "Bobby, if you can do something once, you can do it again." Learning to compensate for my disability was a difficult process, made harder by my own laziness. Whenever I didn't want to do something, I contrived a way to get out of it. My parents, of course, were wise to me, but my teachers (most of whom were older ladies I called fuddy-duddies) were often unsuspecting. God was gracious to me, however, and he used my mother to protect me from pride and self-pity.

~

The occupational therapist at the Center taught feeding, dressing, and typing. Her name was Miss Jensen and she was not one of the unsuspecting fuddy-duddies. She was a tough teacher and she made life hell for everybody, especially me. As early as when I was six years old, I can remember thinking that her face resembled the face of the Wicked Witch of the West in the film version of The Wizard of Oz. In our occupational therapy sessions, we students struggled to defy our damaged brains, but Miss Jensen had high expectations and seemed to have no sympathy. The consensus of opinion among my peers was that she pushed us too hard (the treatment probably did me some good, since

I was so lazy). After about five or six years of Miss Jensen, all of us kids were fed up with her.

One morning, when I was about twelve years old, I slipped a letter opener into my book bag. I didn't know when I might get the chance, but I had made up my mind to kill Miss Jensen. Fortunately, I was too busy that day to do her any harm. Although the intention of my heart was to do evil, God prevented me from carrying out my plan. When I got home from school, my father saw the potential murder weapon in my bag and asked, "Why do you have this?"

"I wanted my friends to see it," I said. Since the letter opener looked like a Spanish sword, my lie seemed to pacify Dad's curiosity. But I noticed that he put the letter opener away in a place beyond my reach.

A few months later, at the school lunch table, a student picked up a knife and lunged at Miss Jensen. In a flash, she jerked him out of his chair. The next thing I knew, he was lying on the floor and Miss Jensen was running, screaming to the office. I squirmed in my chair, terrified but happy. It was a relief to know that somebody else had come up with the same plan I had. Unlike me, however, the poor kid was mentally retarded and couldn't comprehend the consequences of his actions. I did understand the consequences of my actions, however, which only goes to show the evil that was inside my heart.

To this day, I sometimes wonder how I ever managed to leave that place with a sound mind. Ironically, it was Miss Jensen who taught me my most valuable functional skill, typing. Even after years of practice, for me to type a single letter of the alphabet requires intense concentration. I have to insert the little finger of my left hand into the appropriate hole in a special cover called a key guard that fits over the keys of my electric typewriter. My left little finger is the only really controllable part of my hands. The muscles of my other fingers, especially those of my right hand and arm, respond poorly to messages from my brain. Learning how to type gave me the means to communicate creatively and freely and to prove my intelligence to other people. I was a young man, however, before I really understood how useful this was to me.

Even though Miss Jensen was not an easy woman to fool, I never stopped trying. When I was about thirteen years old I began using my electric typewriter at school like a slot machine. I hit the "jackpot" if the coin I dropped into the works disabled the typewriter. I then played dumb about the malfunction and managed to evade a little schoolwork. Most of my classmates were mentally retarded, but they soon caught on and started doing the same thing. I was a bad influence on them.

~

During my early childhood years, I didn't read many books by myself, but enjoyed listening as Mother read aloud from Dr. Seuss, fairy tales, and stories about animals, especially cats. She also read poetry aloud. I frequently requested The Highwayman. In this romantic poem, enemies kidnap a maid in order to trap her bandit lover. In the end, both lovers die. The Highwayman might have made a good opera—that's probably why I liked it so much.

When I finally did begin reading books on my own, I usually selected fairy tales and myths. The Arabian Nights is still one of my favorites. I also enjoyed reading about the lives of various composers, artists, and the history of art. I learned most of my American history by going to Gerald's room and reading a hardcover magazine called American Heritage. During one of those excursions, I discovered his stack of Playboy magazines. I had a pre-pubescent fascination for them, but eventually decided there were more interesting things in Gerald's room to look at, such as our 1956 edition of the World Book Encyclopedia. I spent hours studying the pages of those volumes. Occasionally, I asked Mother to look up something for me (usually about opera or a foreign country), but Mother was never satisfied to simply read the article to me and close the book. She quizzed me on the subject to reinforce my comprehension and recall. I was fortunate to be "home-schooled" in this way.

My parents believed that I was intelligent, and I think it was important to Mother that my teacher should believe it also. She frequently invited my teacher, Miss Cribly, to dinner. This was an important relationship, for I was in Miss Cribly's class, the primary grade, from the time I left the kindergarten class until I was nine years old. During her visits to our home, I never failed to show Miss Cribly the little RCA record player my parents had given me. It had come complete with a set of 45-rpm recordings of classical music. I took special pleasure in playing these recordings for my teacher. Actually, I wasn't able to operate the machine myself. Someone else had to stack the records on the player and turn it on for me.

Mother was wise to open our home to my teacher. I'm sure that what Miss Cribly saw of my activities at home gave insight into my work at school. She was a very understanding woman and patiently deciphered my difficult speech in order to write down the fantastic tales I made up about wicked witches in magic lands, and cats, of all things. We did not own a cat. Miss Cribly, I think, recognized that behind my ridiculous stories and my scribbled drawings was a mind that was quick and capable of reflecting on everyday happenings.

During my last years in the primary grade, when I was seven or eight years old, Mr. Ebert, a music teacher from the Clifton Public Schools, began having a music class at the Cerebral Palsy Center once every three weeks. That wasn't often enough to satisfy my interest. I remember asking Mother about taking some kind of music lessons and one day asking Mr. Ebert if he would give me private lessons at home on the electric organ. I wanted to play operatic and symphonic melodies, so Mr. Ebert transcribed for the organ the music I asked for, little bits of La Traviata, Rigoletto, Carmen, Beethoven, Mozart, and Schubert. For the next five years Mr. Ebert came to my house for private lessons, which usually centered on my interests. He tried introducing some music theory and analysis, but I was not ready to study on a technical level. Besides, the lessons were considered a pastime. Both at school and at home, everyone emphasized the importance of physical therapy and academic performance.

More than anything else I had yet attempted to do, the music lessons gave me the positive sense of uniqueness I needed during the early years of my life and showed other people that I had the intelligence and the motivation to learn something. Even as a child, I sensed that my physical appearance and speech difficulty led people to assume at first glance that I was mentally retarded. But when Miss Cribly and Mr. Ebert responded to me as a person with normal intelligence, I felt I might be worth something to people outside of my immediate family. This was a small beginning, and it was years later before other teachers recognized my intellect. Sadly, to this day, some have never acknowledged it.

~

There were only a few children that I counted as friends at the time. Among them was a girl named Muriel Wild. Everybody at the Cerebral Palsy Center liked Muriel because she was outgoing and talkative. Long after we had all left the Cerebral Palsy Center, when she was 18 or 19 years old, Muriel went to work for Avon selling toiletries. I was her best customer until Dad put his foot down. "No more after-shave," he said. "We have enough now to shave ourselves for forty years!" Muriel continued selling Avon products to other people for years and did so well that the company awarded her a prize.

Another friend of mine was Joann DeGise. Joann was in my class at the Cerebral Palsy Center. Her family was one of the warmest, most loving families I have ever known. Each year they hosted a school picnic at their house in the New

Jersey countryside. (Theirs was one of the first in-ground swimming pools in someone's back yard my father had ever seen. I'm convinced that the DeGise's pool is what started him thinking about someday moving to Florida. We visited the DeGises often and I can easily imagine how tempting it was for Dad to want to sit beside a pool and forget about his business for a while.)

The DeGise home was the closest thing to rural America I experienced during my childhood. It was no farm, but quite different from the urban neighborhood I lived in. I had great fun playing in the woods and the expanses of grass with Joann, her brother and sister. I either crawled on the ground or used a wheelchair borrowed from the school. Animals—cats, dogs, kittens, and puppies—roamed the place. I worked for a long time to convince Mother to let me have one of the DeGise's puppies.

From the time I became old enough to understand that people owned animals as pets, I wanted one. But any talk of keeping pets brought objections from Mother. She was especially set against having animals in the house. She didn't mind, however, if occasionally Aunt Ida sent little turtles from Florida. I took the turtles out of their dish and played with them on the floor. I guess all that handling wasn't good for turtles. Ours never lived longer than a few weeks.

Anna knew how much I wanted a pet and one spring day, she presented me with a shoebox. Inside were baby chicks. They were cute, but their behavior was something else. Two chicks tried pecking each other's eyes out. I was horrified! Mother and Anna put the fighters into separate boxes. That calmed things down, but after a few days I lost interest in the chicks, so Anna took them away.

While I didn't consider turtles and chicks as my pets, I still didn't know what my ideal pet should be. Then I saw a parakeet. I begged for one until Mother gave in. We all went to the pet store on my sixth birthday and I chose a blue parakeet. I named her Tweetie-pie. I liked watching Tweetie-pie eat and play in her cage. She was tame, so my parents often set her free in the house. Just to be on the safe side, so she couldn't fly away, they clipped her wings a little. Sometimes Tweetie-pie sat on Dad's finger. He tried teaching her to talk, but I guess her birdbrain couldn't comprehend what was expected. Sometimes she sat on Mother's shoulder while Mother did the dishes or worked around the house.

One day I decided to take Tweetie-pie out of her cage all by myself. I managed to open the cage and put her on the floor. She hopped away but I caught her. Tweetie-pie was in my hand when I had an involuntary movement. My arms jerked and I slammed the bird to the floor. Tweetie-pie's limp body rolled out of my hand. Mother saw Tweetie-pie and understood at once what had happened. She gently put me to bed. I fell asleep immediately. I knew involuntary movements were something beyond my control, but it took me days to get over the loss of my first pet.

Some time later Mother yielded again and my brother and I shared ownership of a white rabbit. I wanted to name him Whitey, but Gerald said we should call him Flash. Neither he nor I would give in. Gerald built a nice cage and we kept the rabbit inside the house. Whitey-Flash was big and warm and cuddly, but he was not very smart. Every morning I let him out of the cage to play with him, and every morning he went behind the couch and did his business. The day Mother looked behind the couch was the day we sent Whitey-Flash to live on a farm. To make our parting easier, Mother told me the rabbit would be happier in the country. But I wasn't very sad to see him go. I had already made up my mind. My next pet was going to be a dog.

I got the idea for a dog from Joann DeGise. I selected a female from the most recent litter. The pup was nothing but a plain old mutt, but Dad assured Mother that a mutt was the best kind of dog for a young boy. I named her Lulubelle, after the comic book character Little Lulu. She slept in a bed I made from a drawer and some old pillows. When she outgrew her drawer, she slept on my bed with me. Dad and Gerald trained her, so that Lulubelle was always well behaved. We spoiled her, though, and treated her like a member of the family. Whenever we had tomatoes and sour cream or Alderney's ice cream, Lulubelle got her share. Lulubelle also got her share of the teasing. Dad and Gerald's favorite trick was to hold dog biscuits in their hands while Dad called to Lulubelle from the front of the house and Gerald called to her from the back. The poor dog was beside herself with confusion.

Lulubelle turned out to be everything I ever wanted in a pet. And though Mother used to remind us that she had never wanted a dog in the first place, she came to like Lulubelle far more than she ever intended to.

Joann, Muriel and I left the Cerebral Palsy Center at the same time, and I suppose I had enough schooling to account for a sixth grade education. In spite of the inadequacies of my training, I was proud of my academic achievements. That pride, combined with my love for operatic music, convinced me that the world had a lot to offer me. I knew that I had serious physical limitations, but I didn't dwell on them. I was too busy with therapy, studies, and music—the things I could do.

~

There were limits to what I could do, of course, as a physically disabled child, but I did not grow up feeling deprived socially. Besides my schoolmates, I had friendships with neighborhood children. I often sat on the curb watching the boys play ball in the street. They included me in their conversations and told me all of the dumb jokes that kids have always told each other.

When I was five or six years old, I pedaled a white and gold four-wheeled kiddie car along the sidewalk in the neighborhood. The car looked like a jet airplane and I guess it could count as my first wheelchair. Pedaling was easier than walking. Swimming was the only other practical exercise for me. I couldn't do much in the water except hang on to my inner tube and kick my feet, but that was enough. Until I was twelve or thirteen, I usually went to the pool with my brother. Gerald was a big boy, full of horseplay and fun.

He liked to make me hold my breath while he pushed my head under water for a few seconds. I also enjoyed the game, which he claimed was helping me exercise breath control.

Gerald loved to exercise and flex his big muscles. Sports, especially tennis and swimming, occupied most of his time. I had no interest in sports and Gerald had no interest in opera. This was fortunate, because our differences kept me from living in his shadow and becoming dissatisfied with myself because of my limitations. Yet there was a healthy competition between us. I was expected to hold my own—and did—as we constantly provoked each other and pulled boyish pranks. I often watched Gerald play while I was very young. My uncooperative arms and clenched hands prevented me from using many toys myself. He went through a phase of building elaborate Lincoln Log structures. Once I watched him work all morning on a Lincoln Log fort that eventually covered the floor of his small bedroom. Gerald was proud of that fort and wanted to leave it in place until Dad came home from work. But that afternoon, he did something that made me angry. I crawled to his room and scattered the little logs in every direction. Another time I broke one of his 45-rpm recordings of Elvis, this time to pay Gerald back for a practical joke he had pulled on me. Ironically, the title I selected for the hateful deed was *Love Me Tender*.

During construction of an addition to our house, Gerald and I were told we would have to share a bedroom for a few weeks. My fear of falling out of bed magnified this minor adjustment into a major catastrophe. I desperately wanted the bed on the left wall in the room we were to share because I had always slept in a bed arranged against the left wall of the room. I felt secure at night, lying on my right side with my body pressed against the wall. I was afraid that Gerald, whether out of ignorance or out of meanness, would demand first choice of the beds in the new room because he was five years older. Before he could open his mouth, I lunged toward the bed I wanted. I must have looked comical, because instead of argument, I heard Gerald's laughter. I didn't care. I got my bed.

Gerald actually was more understanding than I gave him credit for. Like mother, he was a sociable, good-natured person, always ready to lend a helping hand. He and his friends didn't mind including me in some of their activities, and I went with them to the movies in downtown Passaic nearly every weekend. During The Ten Commandments Gerald and his friends laughed at Yul Brynner's bald head. I fell asleep, but awakened in time to catch the ending. Gerald took me to Snow White, Bambi, and other movies I don't think he really enjoyed. He preferred westerns and adventure films. I loved fantasy, grandeur, and music.

~

In addition to overseeing our schooling, Mother considered it her duty to give my brother and me a strict, moral upbringing. Our family never went to temple, so Mother's teaching was the closest thing to religious training that I had as a child. I remember that in 1957, when I was nine years old, Mother read to me from a comic book called The Ten Commandments. The comic book was based on the film starring Charlton Heston. She had just read, "Honor your father and mother" when I had a forceful involuntary movement and punched the side of her face with my fist. I felt guilty about that for a long time. Now I laugh at the irony.

Though we were not an especially religious family, we did observe some Jewish traditions. Passover was our big family celebration, and Mother and Dad usually invited our relatives to a meal at our house. As with most of our family gatherings, the adults were very vocal. Once I asked why they were all yelling, only to be told, "WE'RE NOT YELLING! WE'RE JUST DISCUSSING LOUDLY!" For the Passover meal we had matzos and chicken and all sorts of delicious food, including shrimp cocktail. I didn't find out until much later in life that shrimp cocktail is not even kosher.

I don't remember having been inside a temple before the morning of Gerald's bar mitzvah in 1954. No one bothered to explain the meaning of the ceremony to me, and I don't think I would have shown any interest even if someone had tried. It wasn't until my mother's death that I slowly began to show interest in God. For us, the event was more social than religious. During the actual ceremony, my attention was mainly attracted to the congregation composed of our relatives and Gerald's friends. It was fascinating to see everyone all dressed up and the men and boys wearing their yarmulkes. I wore a yarmulke, too.

The quiet ceremony was like a prelude to the big celebration that evening at a large reception hall in Patterson. To my mind, the celebration was the bar mitzvah. Dad hired an army of photographers, including movie photographers, to record all the events for posterity. Soon after we arrived, the band began playing the first number and guests converged on the dance floor. There was a luscious buffet. I watched the dance floor antics from my table while Anna fed me all I could eat. Feeding me is not as easy as it sounds. My movements are unpredictable, so getting a spoonful of food into my mouth (while it's open) is a game of skill and chance. I'm not such a tough customer now, but it still can be frustrating at times.

Gerald's bar mitzvah celebration was a dazzling pageant of glittering women in colorful evening gowns, but one of my aunts didn't dress up. She arrived wearing a plain dress. I guess Dad was embarrassed, or wanted to embarrass her, because while she was out on the dance floor he slipped an ice cube down the back of her dress. She jumped and squealed and ran to her table. I didn't see her go back on the dance floor again for the rest of the evening.

This was the year before rock and roll exploded on the music charts, so Gerald and his friends didn't "rock around the clock." They danced the Bunny Hop and the Hokey-Pokey. Dad came over to my table and asked me if

I wanted to dance. It was probably more of a struggle than a dance for Dad, because he physically had to hold me up and every so often my body jerked involuntarily. We didn't know it then, but in about ten years everyone would be dancing that way.

~

In April 1959, just before my eleventh birthday, Mother took me to see my first live performance. It was her favorite opera, *Madama Butterfly*. Since the opera lasted long past my bedtime, I stayed only for the first two acts. I don't remember the names of any of the singers, but I'll never forget the lovely sound of live voices. Mother, on the other hand, was accustomed to the top-quality performances of the Metropolitan Opera. This was only a performance by the New Opera Company of New Jersey, held in an old movie theater in downtown Passaic. During the first act, Mother winced as one of the trees on stage almost fell over. But she was surprised at the soprano, who sang better than expected.

Verdi's *La Traviata* was my favorite opera and it was the last opera I studied with Mother. When a friend of hers once offered to buy me a present, I asked for *La Traviata*. I was presented with Toscanini's recording. Mother was especially pleased and put the new records on the Hi-Fi right away. I now own over a dozen different recordings of *La Traviata*, but none of them gives me the pleasure that Toscanini's does. Mother's favorite part of the opera was the baritone aria, "Di Provenza Il Mar". It seemed that she always hummed this melody. It was my lullaby.

During her own childhood, Mother did not know the warmth and security of a loving family. Her mother died when Mother was very young and her father kept an emotional distance. Mother and her sister Eleanor, however, were close. Sometimes Mother and I went down to Aunt Eleanor's candy store. While I had a treat, Mother caught up on the latest gossip in town. Mother enjoyed hearing about what went on, but Aunt Eleanor usually told more than she needed to know. Despite having experienced a difficult childhood, Mother was kind and gracious to everyone, even to people she did not particularly care for. No wonder Dad's family loved Mother so dearly, and no wonder our home was so happy.

Some of my most beautiful childhood memories are of Mother and Aunt Olga. Actually, Olga was not related to us. I just thought she was. She was Hungarian born, but had grown up in Passaic. As children, she and Mother had become best friends. They remained best friends for life, even after Olga married and moved to Chile. I remember two occasions, years apart, when Olga visited Mother at our home in Passaic. Olga and Mother were very much alike and both full of music. Aunt Olga, with her sweet Hungarian accent, often sang to me. After the first visit, whenever Mother sent a letter to Olga, I included a letter I that I had composed.

In 1959, our family experienced the spring of hope and the winter of despair. Mother was making plans to visit Olga in Chile. Air travel in the late 1950s wasn't as sophisticated as it is now, so the whole idea was quite adventuresome. Mother talked Dad's sister, Ida, into going with her. The preparations were well underway when, in early June with the departure date fast approaching, Mother had a severe physical reaction to the required smallpox vaccination. Her brief illness led our family doctor, Mother's uncle Ben Provisor, to a startling discovery. Mother had leukemia. Uncle Ben told Dad the truth, but they never told Mother how seriously ill she was. I suppose it was better for Mother that way. Believing she would recover kept her from worrying about Gerald and me. But it meant Dad had to carry the burden of despair alone.

The same week Mother got sick, some of my friends were graduating from the Cerebral Palsy Center. On graduation day, Dad came home from work early. I was wearing a tie and jacket and Mother was dressed up, too. She always dressed fashionably. Dad took pictures of Mother and me together; we never guessed that beneath his smile his heart was breaking. I knew Mother wasn't well, but assumed it was because of the vaccination. Mother attended the graduation with me, but partway through the ceremony she told me she didn't feel well and needed to see Uncle Ben. I guess she called Dad, because he picked her up at the school and drove her to Uncle Ben's office. When the program ended, Dad was waiting to take me home. The other adults at the graduation seemed to know something I didn't know. I sensed the tension, was frightened and cried. Dad told me not to worry and took me home and put me to bed. I was still awake when Mother's taxi stopped in front of the house. I heard the cab door slam and I heard her footsteps echo in the night as she came up the walk. She stayed in bed all the next day.

Partly to protect me and partly to ease his own grief, Dad arranged for me to stay with various neighbors, friends, and relatives for the next few weeks. They couldn't keep everything from me, but no one ever told me the truth. When I asked, "How's Mommy doing?" Dad would just say, "She still doesn't feel well."

In July, I went to a summer camp for the handicapped. At the end of the three-week session, Dad came to take me home. The first thing I asked him was, "Is Mommy OK?"

This time he said, "No. I'll tell you what happened when we get home."

Once we got settled inside our house, Dad said, "Something happened that doesn't happen to people very often, but it happened to Mother." He said something about a disease, but I didn't understand because my brain was spinning too fast and it didn't stop until I heard Dad pause before he said, ". . . and that's how she died."

It may seem strange, but I was not angry with Dad for having waited so long to tell me. I somehow understood that he had needed time to get himself under control before he could tell me the truth and comfort me. He hugged me until I stopped crying. Lulubelle was with us. Dad said that even the dog felt lost without Mother.

Two months passed before I asked Dad to describe Mother's last days. He gave me a little information, but it was still too painful for him to discuss in any detail. Aunt Ida, Dad's sister, had come from Miami and was staying with us for a while, so I asked her. She told me that Dad and other relatives had cared for Mother at home until the night she went into a coma. Dad was with her when it happened. And he was with her when she died at the hospital 24 hours later, on Thursday, June 25, 1959.

I was barely eleven years old when Mother died. I didn't question why she was taken from me. Death, I knew, was something human beings could not change. But after Mother's death, something inside me changed. I started wondering what happened to people after they died. As a result, with little teaching to guide me, I began believing in God. Looking back, it seems that from that time on, something imperceptible drew me toward Him.

CHAPTER 2

Another Mother

Now that I was back home, Dad was immediately faced with the problem of finding someone to take care of me while he was at work. Aunt Ida was still with us, but she needed to return to her own family in Miami. When September finally came and I could spend the whole day at school, it was a relief to everyone, including me. Spending the days at home, where Mother had always been close at hand, gave me no escape from my intense feeling of loss. Returning to school helped me to move on emotionally.

Dad depended on Anna to stay with me after school until he came home from work. She had the weekends off, so on Saturdays, while Dad and Gerald worked at the lumberyard that was the family business, Aunt Eleanor's daughter Gail stayed with me. Sometimes, an old Italian woman named Betty from the Cerebral Palsy Center came on a Saturday and took me to an amusement park or to visit a classmate. These arrangements worked fairly well, but Dad knew he couldn't continue to depend on other people to take care of his family. I needed a mother. I think that was one reason my father started looking for a suitable wife, but I know it was not his primary reason. He couldn't stand being single.

Charlotte Brawer had been a widow for eight years. She lived in Fair Lawn, New Jersey, and made a comfortable living for herself and her two children by selling mutual funds. Dad had lived in Passaic all of his life and knew practically everyone in the old Jewish community. He had heard about Charlotte from her cousin, who also lived in Passaic. It is said that I charmed Charlotte into marrying my father. I admit that I played an important role in their romance, but I think the claim is an exaggeration. Nevertheless, it is true that Charlotte was intrigued by my unusual interest in classical music and opera. I, on the other hand, was attracted by her vast knowledge of literature. Charlotte had the air of an English teacher, which I suppose she had inherited from her father, who had taught English and had written a grammar book.

Dad, Gerald, and I began spending every weekend with Charlotte and her children, Irvene and Barney. Irvene was younger than Gerald was. Barney and I were both twelve. Like Charlotte, Barney had an impressive knowledge of literature and music. He also had an obnoxious sense of humor that I thought was wonderful. Irvene, Barney, and Charlotte read the news headlines every day and carried on heated debates about everything. All three were very opinionated and the broad range of the topics they discussed amazed me. Up until then, I had never given a thought to politics, cultures, and events beyond my own neighborhood and family. The Brawers shocked me into realizing I was part of a larger world.

As time went on, Irvene and Gerald, being older teenagers, preferred to be with their own friends on the weekends. Barney and I were left with Dad and Charlotte. We usually went to a movie, show, or museum in New York City. Sometimes we visited relatives—either Charlotte's or Dad's. One thing was constant: our day ended with a big dinner. If we didn't go to a restaurant, Dad and Charlotte cooked something at either Charlotte's house in Fair Lawn or at our house in Passaic. Dad, not Charlotte, was really the one who loved to cook. Perhaps because Mother's culinary skill had spoiled him, he hated to settle for mediocre meals and after Mother died, he, Gerald, and I took over the kitchen. Under Dad's leadership, the three of us turned out to be excellent cooks. I didn't do the physical work of cooking, but I studied the recipes like a roadmap and gave directions like a back seat driver. I still do.

Charlotte and Dad were married in 1961. The fact that my father was able to court a lady, manage his growing lumber business, and care for me all at the same time is a testimony to his indomitable spirit. Next to my father and Charlotte, I was the happiest of the bunch. But it was not so easy for Gerald, Barney, and Irvene. They had trouble becoming one big happy family.

I was unaware of their struggles. Gerald, the athlete, could never understand how Barney could be content to do nothing but read books and newspapers. Barney, who was advanced in his studies, thought changing from the school in Fair Lawn to the school in Passaic was taking a step down. He was not happy until Charlotte sent him to a better high school in New York City. Irvene was upset about leaving the school in Fair Lawn too, but agreed to finish high school in Passaic. Unfortunately, she had to live in the upstairs hallway until an additional bedroom and office could be added on to our house. Now that I understand what she went through, I couldn't blame Irvene for any bitter feelings she might have had. Fortunately, it didn't take very long for my brothers and sister to learn to love and respect one another. But it's no exaggeration to say that I was the child who benefited the most from Dad and Charlotte's marriage.

Charlotte continued to work full-time, so we still needed a housekeeper and someone to help care for me after school. Anna had been with us for years, but after Mother's death, she became possessive about the house and, when Charlotte moved in, temperamental. Anna and Charlotte never could get along and we began a cycle of Anna "quitting for good" yet always coming back. This situation compounded the strain the members of my family were under, since when we were without a housekeeper, each had to take a turn staying with me after school.

This went on until one day, Charlotte's friend Esther mentioned a young woman she knew of in Denmark who wanted to live with an American family for a year. Charlotte grabbed at the opportunity with both hands.

Beautiful, blonde, blue-eyed Ingrid came to live with us at the end of August 1962. When I saw her it was love at first sight. I think my father was taken in by her looks, too, and her presence in our home occasionally caused some confusion. Soon after she came to us, Ingrid drove Dad's Corvette to the bank. She went inside, did her banking, and left. The teller who had helped her knew that Dad had remarried, but hadn't yet seen the new wife. A few minutes after Ingrid's departure, my father entered the bank. The teller said, "Oh, your wife was just in here."

"My wife?"

"Yes. A nice blonde driving the Corvette."

Dad left the bank chuckling. He never did set the teller straight.

In Denmark, Ingrid had taught mentally retarded children. Her professional experience translated into the diligent care she gave me. Each morning she put me through the exercises my physical therapist recommended and every afternoon she helped me with my homework.

Ingrid spoke English very well. Our conversations opened my eyes about life in her native culture. I listened in awe as Ingrid described the surrender of Denmark to German occupation during World War II. During the first weeks of occupation, the Danish people hid their entire Jewish population and ferried them all secretly in fishing boats to neutral Sweden. Ingrid had been close to my own age when she had witnessed these events. Hearing her account made a strong impression on me and gave me great respect for the courage of the Danes. Our discussions about Jews led to a few discussions about Jesus Christ. Ingrid's knowledge was sketchy, because she regarded Jesus only as an historical figure, yet that information planted the first seeds of the Christian faith in my heart.

Ingrid loved exploring New York City and so did I. The fact that I was in a wheelchair limited the number of places we could go together, but Ingrid determined to find ways to get around the obstacles. At bus stops, for example, she boldly asked other passengers to lift me on or off the bus. People were always obliging and time after time we rode confidently into the city to see museums, concerts, Broadway shows, operas, movies, or just go shopping on the avenues.

One time she was pushing me across Fifth Avenue. Right in the middle of the crosswalk my front wheels hit a bump. The jolt threw me onto the street. Ingrid and I were completely taken by surprise, but within seconds people surrounded us, snatched me off the street, and put me back in my wheelchair. It happened so quickly that it almost seemed I had bounced back into my seat. I was dirty, but was not injured. Though Ingrid and I were choking with laughter, she kept her head and we reached the sidewalk before the light changed.

My year with Ingrid passed quickly for all of us. I had been having too much fun and taking too much for granted to notice the question hanging over my family. It was, of course, the question of how to take care of me after Ingrid went home. Dad and Charlotte had been struggling to come up with an answer all year.

They wanted a solution that offered me the best opportunity they could provide. My doctors led them to believe that given enough time and enough therapy, there was a real chance I could live an independent life. I suppose independence must have seemed like a remote possibility, because I seldom did anything for myself that I didn't want to do. Charlotte suspected as much. Soon after she married my father, she set about to find out exactly how much I was capable of doing. Charlotte was successful in business because she was strong-willed and determined. Unfortunately, these characteristics often drove her to maternal extremes. In the same way that she had always pushed Irvene and Barney, she pushed me to do everything for myself that I could. But no matter how hard Charlotte leaned on me, I wouldn't pick up her momentum.

In spite of my passivity, her past observation of me had convinced Charlotte that I had normal intelligence. She also recognized that the education I was receiving at the Cerebral Palsy Center would never develop my intellectual potential. With Dad's approval, she began searching for a better school. Ideally, this school would offer the therapy I needed and challenge me academically. She had never heard of such a school for cerebral palsied children, but if one existed, she intended to find it.

After I graduated from the Cerebral Palsy Center and until Charlotte could find the right school for me, my parents decided to place me in an institution where I could receive intensive physical therapy. I took the decision in stride. I was thirteen years of age and, having previously attended summer camps for the handicapped, had already experienced leaving home. Most importantly, I clearly understood Dad and Charlotte's reasoning.

The doctor in charge of the Cerebral Palsy Center recommended Dr. Winthrop Phelps' "school" near Baltimore, Maryland. We already knew Dr. Phelps, an orthopedic surgeon, because he and various other doctors regularly held clinics at the Cerebral Palsy Center. Dr. Phelps had prescribed braces for me, as well as phenobarbital, the first of many medications I took to control involuntary movements. He was an older gentleman whose bald head, black suit and black tie, and kindly manner reminded me of a Civil War-era southern aristocrat. Because Dr. Phelps was a man I trusted, I looked forward with a sense of adventure to "going away to school."

Dr. Phelps' school was a big, old farmhouse divided into two sections, one for boys and one for girls. Therapy areas and classrooms were on a level above the main floor. The basement served as a cafeteria, although a more appropriate term might be "mess hall," because it literally was a mess. Every room in the building smelled of urine. Charlotte later described the place as a snake pit.

I lived on a ward with both children and adults who were of either normal intelligence or mentally retarded. Fortunately, neither Dr. Phelps nor his staff treated me as if I was mentally retarded. Because I occupied my time by reading books and magazines or playing Mother's records, they recognized that I had some intelligence.

I was generally a quiet, well-behaved boy, but like the other patients on the ward, I was bored. One day I saw that the boy in the bed next to mine had a bag of candy. Our beds were on wheels, so I reached across the space between us and pulled my bed next to his. He watched helplessly while I grabbed his candy bag and quickly stuffed a few pieces into my mouth. When he screamed I pushed my bed away, so that the identity of the guilty one wouldn't immediately be obvious to the nurses. At the time, I wasn't ashamed to be scolded. I thought it to be a harmless, childish caper meant to stir up excitement. Stealing candy from a mentally handicapped child was a pretty rotten thing to do, however, and just as my desire to murder my occupational therapist, Ms. Jensen, was sin, this theft was also sinful. I needed the grace of God even at this young age.

My occasional pranks could not overcome the overall effect of bland, institutional life. I now realize it was a miracle of God that I survived the experience with my personality intact. Too quickly, I grew accustomed to the long periods of boredom that followed scheduled activities. I made no effort to do anything for myself, but withdrew into my own private, passive world. I waited to be taken out of bed. Waited to be fed. Waited to be taken to the bathroom. Waited to be told what to do next.

One thing at the school, however, had a positive effect on me. I discovered the Bible. Every week a nun from a local convent held classes for the Catholic patients. The things she said about God and Jesus Christ fascinated me. Being Jewish, I had never really heard anything about Christ except what Ingrid had told me, and that was vague.

One day the boy in the bed next to mine threw away a book of Bible stories. I rescued the book and kept it for quite a while. This was my first encounter with the New Testament. I read Bible stories every night and was soon answering questions in the nun's class. I kept the book hidden from Dad and Charlotte, because I knew that they thought religion was a waste of time.

As I grew taller my balance grew worse. I walked less and depended on a wheelchair more. Constant sitting caused the muscles in the back of my legs to shrink. Dr. Phelps warned that the deformity would become permanent and said I would never walk again unless he did something to straighten my legs. One technique that Phelps and other orthopedic specialists used to relieve tightened, palsied muscles required surgery. Sometimes this procedure improved the condition and sometimes it did not. I now know that many cerebral palsied persons suffered a great deal because they allowed themselves to be operated on without questioning the ideas behind surgical procedures. In those days, however, people were awed by a physician's credentials and did as they were told. My parents were too smart for that—at least when my mother was alive. She refused to allow anyone to operate on me. Dad also was inclined to exhaust every possibility before resorting to surgery, so instead of having an operation to straighten my legs, I was strapped into heavy, full-length leg braces. The braces were terribly confining, but at least I only had to wear them for a few hours each day.

Charlotte was determined to help me improve my physical condition and went about it with the fury of a hurricane, which was the only way she knew to get things done. I remember coming home from Maryland for a vacation and being tied by Charlotte to the wrought iron banister of the stairs leading to the second floor of our house. I had full-length braces on my legs and this forced me to use my trunk muscles to hold my body upright. It was impossible for me to maintain this posture. When I slumped forward, Charlotte scolded me and told me to stand up straight. I did not have the upper body strength or the coordination to do what she wanted. I begged her to take me down. When she refused to give in, I started screaming, "GO TO HELL!" Charlotte ignored me. I yelled every obscenity and wicked thing I could think of, but Charlotte held firm until Dad came home from work. He untied me and took off those horrible braces. I suppose the entire incident lasted only thirty minutes. It seemed like hours to me.

After nine months of having kept me at Dr. Phelps' rehabilitation center, my father was disgusted. In his opinion, I was going nowhere fast. Charlotte was irritated with me because I had picked up the habit of passively waiting for everything to be done for me. I was unaware of it, but Dad and Charlotte struggled with the whole idea of subjecting me to physical therapy and rehabilitation centers. They questioned, for example, why my therapists kept talking about walking when I was dependent on a wheelchair, and why I was being educated in the same classroom with the mentally retarded when I had a good mind.

Dad and Charlotte were looking for new hope. They decided to take me to the respected Institute of Physical Medicine and Rehabilitation in New York City for an evaluation. The Institute is often referred to as the Rusk Institute, after its founder and director Dr. Howard Rusk, a world-famous authority on treating the disabled. Dr. Rusk had distinguished himself as a pioneer in the field of rehabilitation medicine with his emphasis on treating the "whole man." He lectured throughout the world and had published works such as New Hope for the Handicapped (1949). The Rusk Institute's reputation was such that Joseph Kennedy, father of President Kennedy, had gone there for treatment after his stroke in 1961. At the Rusk Institute, I was to have a complete physical and psychological evaluation.

In the meantime, Charlotte wanted me to do everything I could for myself, no matter how long it took. I did not fully understand her reasoning, but she made it clear to me and to everyone in the family that if I needed something, I would have to take the initiative to get it. Charlotte meant business. One morning she didn't come to my room to get me out of bed. I knew it was time to get up, so I called for help and I waited. Charlotte was waiting too. She wanted to see how long it would take me to get angry enough to do something—to do anything. I didn't even call a second time. Four hours later, Charlotte stormed into my room. "BOB!" I snapped out of my stupor. She was right in front of my face. "Listen to me," she said. "I don't want you to become one of those numb-skulls like we saw in Maryland! They have no initiative! No drive! No intelligence! You have all of these things and I don't want you to lose them. It's time you started using the abilities you have." I knew Charlotte was right, but I just couldn't understand that I would have to take the initiative.

Consequently, I was a passive subject during my evaluation at the Rusk Institute and left all decisions and concern about the results to my parents.

CHAPTER 3

We Should Have Known Better

by
Charlotte Brawer-Kaplowitz

When sixteen-year-old Bob came home at the end of a four-month long evaluation at the Rusk Institute, he had nothing to show for the ordeal except a watercolor painting and this estimation of his human potential: "He has none."

Sitting in his wheelchair at home in his room, Bob watched me unpack his things. "What do you want me to do with this painting?" I asked.

"Tell the Committee the truth."

The Committee, President Kennedy's Committee for the Handicapped, unwittingly had awarded the brush-strokes of the occupational therapist who had presented the painting as the work of Bob's own hand. The President's Committee didn't see Bob's contracted, wasted hands. They didn't see his arms jerk involuntarily. If they had, they would have known better.

Bob hasn't enough coordination to write his own name, much less paint something recognizable. How could anyone pretend Bob had painted a prize-winning picture and then declare he had no potential as a human being?

"No," I said. "Those people have hurt us enough. Let's just let sleeping dogs lie."

The reason Bob's father and I had turned to NYU's Institute of Physical Medicine and Rehabilitation in New York City was because we had been told that its outstanding authorities on cerebral palsy would give Bob the most comprehensive examination possible. Naturally, Jack and I had high expectations regarding the outcome of the exam. It would of course verify what we already knew, that Bob had a quick mind and an engaging personality. It would also settle once and for all whether or not continued physical therapy would enable Bob to retain the limited walking ability that he now had with braces and a cane. On top of our confidence, we had sufficient naivete to hope for advice and assistance in finding a residential center where Bob could receive a good education.

Dr. Leon Greenspan of the Children's Department met with us first and examined Bob. A complete evaluation, he said, would take several months. Bob must live at the Institute the entire time, but might come home for an occasional weekend. Dr. Greenspan warned us that the evaluation would be costly. The exact charge, however, could not be predicted, since it depended on how much physical, mental, and psychological testing Bob actually required. In spite of the uncertainty, we agreed to everything.

Bob entered the hospital in his usual good spirits and immediately became one of the staff favorites. How Bob, a gangly, twisted adolescent, managed to compete with the adorable tots on his ward I will never know, but he did. Those darling little children were seeking help for all sorts of disabling conditions: cerebral palsy, muscular dystrophy, birth defects, amputations, illnesses, and injuries.

I'll never forget my shock at my first sight of children being fitted with artificial hands. In a short while, though, I got used to seeing a two or three-year old child with hooks where hands should have been. I learned to ignore the problems, to greet the children, to joke with them, to laugh. Most of the children were in good spirits when visitors were about. What they were like at other times I could not know. The nurses and doctors were unfailingly kind and cheerful. They always had time for a few words of recognition, encouragement, and approval.

During Bob's stay, we got to know two other teens fairly well. One, a girl about Bob's age, had been in a water-skiing accident. She had fallen into the path of a boat and in one horrible instant its propeller had severed both legs at the thigh. What wonderful spirit she had. She was lovely, optimistic, and happy. How beautiful it was to see such courage.

Then there was Juan, Bob's roommate. Several years earlier, Dr. Rusk had been on a speaking tour in South America. Unknown to him, several convent nuns in Bolivia were raising a seriously malformed child who had been found as an infant in a garbage can and brought to them. When the nuns heard that a famous American doctor was in the area, they pleaded with him to see the boy. Dr. Rusk did, and brought Juan to the United States for treatment.

When Bob arrived at the Institute, Juan had been living there for several years and now spoke excellent English. During the week, Juan lived at the Institute and went to a special school from there. He spent most of his weekends, however, at the home of a doctor who had adopted him. One day Irvene and Barney decided to visit Bob. I was afraid they might be shocked when they saw Juan and tried to prepare them. "Juan has a lovely head and face and is delightful to talk to," I told them. "And his body is fine. But he has no legs, not even the beginnings of a thigh. And he has no arms. He has three finger-like appendages at each shoulder and with those fingers he can do many things—even write by twisting his body and holding his shoulder close to the paper." Irvene and Barney accepted the information without comment and went on their way. They came home from the hospital full of enthusiasm and went back to visit Bob and Juan many times.

Bob's father and I also made regular trips in to see Bob. But after months of commuting from our home in New Jersey to visit Bob in New York City; after months of watching the smiling doctors and nurses go up and down the familiar halls; we began wondering why in the world it was taking so long to analyze Bob's condition. We could not get the slightest clue as to what they were testing, or how, or when. Everyone we asked avoided our questions. "We can't give you the results until we've completed all the tests," they said. They gave not a word to either encourage or discourage us. It was all pleasant conversation—but not a shred of information. Our patience was running out.

Finally, the examination was complete. Bob's father and I sat in Dr. Greenspan's office, eager to hear the report which we felt certain would confirm our own observations. Right away we wanted to know, "Will more physical therapy improve Bob's ability to walk?"

In the most patronizing manner, Dr. Greenspan told us it made little difference whether or not Bob wore braces and continued physical therapy. "In fact," he said, "in Israel cerebral palsied children are not even given physical therapy."

Already we suspected that forcing Bob to walk was not worth the effort, but we were stunned by Dr. Greenspan's attitude. When speaking to me, he used the Yiddish word "bubbele"—little darling—at the end of every phrase.

He steered the conversation past the intellectual, psychological, and social test results and said, "In my opinion, this boy has too many physical problems to remain at home. Caring for him there would place too much strain on the rest of the family. The best thing for you is put him in one of those places." And then, as if speaking to children about a cherished old doll, he mentioned a place in Kansas where they "kept" people like Bob.

"Just what kind of places are you talking about?" I asked. "And who runs them?"

"They are residential homes. People who have retarded, cerebral palsied children sometimes board several other cerebral palsy cases."

"Do these people have a program of activities for the children?"

"Well, probably not," he said. "Considering the mental capacities of the patients, it's doubtful."

"But don't they have classes for those who are capable of learning?"

Dr. Greenspan leaned toward me. "Bubbele . . . what's the point?"

We listened in horror. "Are you telling us our son has no potential of any kind?" Jack demanded. "That we should leave him somewhere to sit and rot?"

"Well, truthfully, I don't see any other possibility." How could it be? Weren't we paying these doctors thousands of dollars? Did they not see Bob's quick, understanding mind? Hear his spontaneous humor? I admit that his speech is often unclear, but he repeats his words until he is understood. How could anyone be so blind and deaf?

I knew beyond a shadow of doubt that Bob had a well—functioning brain—imaginative, expressive, and observant. I had received letters typed with his own hand while he was away at a summer camp for the handicapped and the rehabilitation center in Maryland. I knew the painstaking effort required for him to type a single letter of the alphabet. I knew the difficulty of turning a series of separate thoughts into a piece of orderly, flowing prose on the first draft. Yet, from the time I met him when he was twelve years old, Bob could unfailingly produce a letter full of comment, flavored with his inimitable humor, remembering to include questions to which he needed answers, and all without disrupting the charm, rhythm, and sequence of the letter. I never saw a P.S. tacked on at the end (as my letters always have) because he failed to include an item in its proper place. How could anyone expect us to believe Bob had no potential when we had solid proof that his mind could remember and organize material without notes or reminders?

Jack and I could only conclude what was clearly the truth. These doctors were so immersed in the mechanics of medicine, muscles, and motion that they ignored the most important thing of all: the mind.

CHAPTER 4

A Time to Give Up

When I returned home from the Rusk Institute I was unaware that Dr. Greenspan had advised my parents to give up on me. Charlotte didn't tell me the details of that conversation until years later. I knew only that Dad and Charlotte were making arrangements to send me to the D. T. Watson Home near Pittsburgh, Pennsylvania. The Home, Charlotte told me, had an accredited high school.

On the day Dad turned our car into the driveway of the well-landscaped D. T. Watson Home, he, Charlotte, and I felt optimistic. This beautiful Home, affectionately named Sunny Hill, turned out to be my home for the next two and a half years. The medical director, Dr. Jessie Wright, had earned a distinguished reputation treating polio and cerebral palsy with physical therapy. My parents were pleased with the facility and returned to Passaic with confidence. I was sixteen years old.

I was sitting in my room when I caught sight of Dr. Wright approaching me. She was an elderly woman with the appearance and voice of a man. This was the first time I had seen her and I was taken aback. Dr. Wright began to examine me, but she paid more attention to my body than she did to my mind. After she finished, I heard her mutter to her assistant under her breath, "Well, we'll see how we can help him," and she left my room without another word. Two days later I found myself being fitted for long leg braces and a back brace. Dismayed, I wondered how she expected me to function in everyday life with these heavy, horrible things on.

Somehow, I had gotten the erroneous impression that my days of wearing braces were over. Little did I know.

Dr. Wright was just getting started. Eventually she added the crowning touch, a head brace. Under her care, I felt like I was being transformed from a human being into a living robot with a body and legs of steel.

In spite of what I went through at the D. T. Watson Home, I am convinced that most of the people who worked there sincerely wanted to help handicapped children. The reputation of the Home bears this out. In fact, in 1952, long before I arrived at the Home, the very first human experiments with the polio vaccine that Dr. Jonas Salk conducted were done on volunteers from the staff and patients of D.T. Watson. The Home made a notable effort to provide schooling and activities for the children. Within that framework, my interests found expression. During a rhythm class program, for example, I played "Climb Every Mountain" on my electric organ. I also submitted to the school newsletter a short theme about the Guiseppe Verdi operas based on Shakespeare's plays. Although I never became accomplished on the organ, many years later I developed the Verdi/Shakespeare theme into a lengthy paper.

Nevertheless, Dr. Wright wrote in my medical record that I was "mildly retarded" and treated me that way. I'm certain the introversion I had developed in Maryland did nothing to enhance my demeanor. When I was not involved in therapy, a class, or an activity, I sat alone, listening to classical music and opera recordings on my little Hi-Fi.

Ann Gray, director of the Speech Therapy Department, however, was one person at D.T. Watson who treated the patients as human beings with minds to be developed as well as bodies. Sometimes she openly criticized what Dr. Wright and Lucille Cochran, the administrator, were doing. Miss Gray encouraged me during speech therapy to voice my opinions, no matter how irrelevant they were. One day I confided to her that it unsettled me to hear the other workers complaining about everything. Miss Gray closed the door to the room and said privately, "Bob, ignore what they say. They just have diarrhea of the mouth." She wanted me to know that she was on my side. The phrase "diarrhea of the mouth" caught my attention and helped me see that I didn't have to take the conversation of the workers too seriously. Still, it was impossible for me to ignore the negative talk.

Many times Dad drove the six hours from Passaic to Pittsburgh to visit me. One weekend, seeing that I was bored, he suggested going to see Gerald. We left my braces at the Home and drove carefree to the University of Cincinnati where Gerald was studying business. We cracked jokes the whole way, but underneath the laughter I sensed my father's concern. I knew he had been leaving the decisions about me up to Charlotte, because she was looking for a better school for me.

I was excited about seeing Gerald and I was excited about meeting Nancy Cohen, an art student and special friend of Gerald's. Nancy had written several letters to me, telling me about herself and about the things she and Gerald did at the university. When I saw Gerald and Nancy together, something inside told me that my brother had found the girl he wanted to marry. Nancy's cheerful, easy-going nature complemented Gerald, who could be impatient and stubborn at times. Dad and I liked Nancy very much and hoped my intuition about a wedding was correct.

Soon the weekend was over and I was back in the braces again.

~

The father of one of my younger classmates at the Home was a rabbi. He lived nearby and came to visit his seven-year-old daughter every week. When Rabbi Jacobs discovered that I was Jewish, he occasionally took me to the service at temple on the Sabbath. My parents were pleased that I had made the acquaintance of a Rabbi. When they came to visit me, they asked to meet him.

One thing led to another and one Saturday morning Dad, Charlotte, and I attended a service at Rabbi Jacobs' temple. This was a miracle of miracles, for Dad and Charlotte went to temple only for a bar mitzvah, a wedding, or a funeral. It so happened that whenever my parents took me on an outing, they left my braces at the Home. That Saturday morning at the service, Rabbi Jacobs was surprised to see how much easier it was to handle me without my braces on. He mentioned it to my parents and they asked Dr. Wright if I could remove my braces whenever the Rabbi took me out. She refused to allow it. She believed I needed the braces in order live a "normal" life.

In addition to Sabbath services, Rabbi Jacobs took me to a concert and a Passover service. Judaism represented tradition to Dad and Charlotte. They did not impart to me a sense of belonging to a people. They did not even observe the Jewish holidays. Rabbi Jacobs included me in his congregation and taught me about Jewish history, the Jewish Bible, and other religions of the world. Though the Rabbi taught me about religion and about God, he did not stress the consequences of personal sin or the impossibility of loving God with all my heart, soul, and strength. My religious feelings, therefore, were expressed in a growing sense of pride in my Jewish ancestry.

During that year, an employee of the Home told me about the Bible she believed in, a Bible that contained both the Old and New Testaments. (I had already learned about that Bible in the Catholic classes in Maryland.) This woman was always talking to me about Jesus Christ. Interested, I bought a King James Bible from her. This disturbed my father. He didn't think I should make decisions about religion yet. He said, "Right now, therapy is more important for you to think about than religion." I gave the Bible back to the woman and Dad bought me a Jewish Bible to replace it. He gave me permission to continue my studies with Rabbi Jacobs if I wanted, but nothing else. It turned out to be a wise decision. Soon afterwards, the woman who sold me the Bible got into an argument with one of the other employees and was fired. The incident left everyone with a bad impression of both her and her religion. Though this woman and her Bible passed out of my life, Jesus Christ did not. I didn't know it, but He would, in His own time, reveal Himself to me.

One of the boys my age at the Home was from Bogota, Columbia. Like me, Pepe had cerebral palsy and normal intelligence. In addition to English, Pepe spoke Italian, Spanish, and German. I was glad when he asked to be my roommate, because it was hard to find anyone with whom I could have a normal conversation. We were typical adolescent boys. We talked mostly about girls.

I rarely asserted myself and never demanded that my needs be met. I passively waited until the workers found time for me. Institutional life had the same effect on Pepe, yet he had a determination to succeed that I did not possess. He somehow forced himself to function with the heavy orthopedic braces Dr. Wright had prescribed for him. I was still trying to find an easy way out. I thought those braces were inhumane contraptions, and I fought them. Consequently, I did not progress as Pepe did. He left the Home about a year after I arrived.

After nine months of therapy, Dr. Wright decided the hamstring on my right leg needed to be surgically released. The muscle was permanently contracted, making it impossible for me to fully straighten my leg or to walk. This was a common surgical procedure, probably the same one Dr. Phelps had recommended for me earlier.

I agreed to the operation, but I was not looking forward to it. I remembered years earlier when fourteen-year old Muriel, my grade school friend from the Cerebral Palsy Center in Clifton, had received a similar operation. Muriel had wept openly when she learned that she would have the procedure. The operation straightened her legs maybe, but I couldn't see the point. She still needed a wheelchair to get around.

Now it was my turn to be victimized by the same procedure. Dr. Wright agreed to allow my doctor in New Jersey to perform the surgery. That gave me an intermission from the soap opera at the Home and allowed me to spend the summer with my family. My parents invited Ingrid to come from Denmark for the summer to take care of me, both before and after the surgery. The first part of the summer was a restful, happy reunion with Ingrid, one of the few people outside my immediate family who sincerely cared about me. We went often to New York City to the usual shows, museums and movies. Dad and Ingrid and I attended a spectacular revival performance of The King and I at the Lincoln Center.

When it was time for my surgery, I entered the hospital in good spirits. Only the anticipation of anesthesia made me apprehensive. I was routinely put under anesthesia for dental work. The ether relaxed my jaw muscles and was supposed to prevent me from involuntarily biting the dentist. I think I bit a few anyway. I hated anesthesia because ether gave me pounding headaches that lasted for hours.

My first words to Dad in the recovery room were, "Where's Ingrid?" My affection for her was very strong. Ingrid took care of me during the last eight weeks of the summer while my leg was in a cast. Then it was time for her to return to Denmark and for me to return to the Home. In parting, she said, "Now it's your turn to visit me."

~

Right away Dr. Wright let me know she was disgusted with my doctor in New Jersey. Before I had returned to the Home, he had removed the top part of my cast. Dr. Wright thought my leg was not as straight as it should have been. I was getting rather disgusted myself, with both her and with the D.T. Watson Home. First of all, Pepe had gone back to Bogota and my new roommate was mentally retarded. I might as well have been in a room by myself. Second, the discord among the staff members kept me in emotional turmoil. And third, there was that head brace.

My leg and back braces were uncomfortable enough, but the head brace Dr. Wright made me wear was torment. The only parts of my body I could move freely were my eyes and arms. The brace held my neck rigid, so that everything

I did had to be at eye level. Anna Grace Lewis, principal of the school department, tried to encourage me by raising my typewriter to eye level so I could at least type. But after a few weeks of straining to type that way and forever slipping my head out of that stupid brace, I gave up. Dr. Wright even strapped weighted cuffs onto my wrists to inhibit my involuntary movements. Ironically, the heavy weights made my arms stronger. Braced and weighted, it was impossible for me to do anything, so I just sat back, numbly waiting to be cared for at the convenience of the staff.

And that is how Charlotte found me when she came to visit. That confrontation was one of the most unpleasant of my life. She was furious because I had stopped trying. She severely scolded me for being passive and for not progressing. "You're seventeen years old. Do you want to be like this for the rest of your life?" she demanded. Charlotte's words put the fear of God in me. I almost felt like I was going to be excommunicated from my family if I didn't begin to show some initiative. After that visit, I made up my mind to give myself wholeheartedly to overcoming my physical limitations. It was a frustrating attempt. Even when I put all of my effort into the therapy, the results were disappointing.

The memory of Charlotte's visit that weekend has had a lasting effect on my life as a Christian. Today, I am constantly surrounded by young men, many of whom struggle with the same sins of laziness and passivity that I had when I was young. It is very difficult for me to watch these men waste time and become passive, and I have been known to confront them on more than one occasion. I didn't know this at the time, but God used Charlotte in my life as an adolescent to prepare me to minister to the young men who would later care for me in my home.

One day I was taken to a treatment room where Dr. Wright was waiting for me. I assumed, since I couldn't turn my head to look around the room and see what she had planned, that she was going to adjust my braces. She began by wrapping my head and head brace with a soft cotton bandage. Then I felt her apply something like plaster on top of that. The realization shook me to the core. She was binding my head to the brace with a cast. I would be mummified until she decided to take this thing off! How long might that be? Had she forgotten that there was a person underneath these steel braces?

The head brace and cast were meant to strengthen my neck muscles so I could hold my head erect. I have to question Dr. Wright's judgment behind this treatment. To this day, I doubt she accomplished anything by it. I still can't hold my head erect for very long.

After the cast was set, I lay in my room for three weeks, dosed at intervals with painkillers or with soup or with baby food. Most of the time I was alone, oblivious to everything, mortified by what she had done to me.

When Dr. Wright cut through the plaster and pulled off the now filthy cotton bandage, she revealed a large open sore on the side of my head. The cast, pressing against my skull, had cut off blood circulation to part of my scalp, destroying the flesh. Dr. Wright swabbed the ulcer with medicine and applied a dressing. She expected it to stay in place. It did not. When the head nurse came in and saw the loose bandage and the bloody mess on my pillow, she snarled, "I have no use for you." I didn't know what to do or what to say. I wanted to snarl, "I have no use for you, either!" but said nothing.

A few days later, I vomited and the bandage had to be changed again. This time Miss Cochran, the administrator, changed it. While she was struggling to position the bandage, I had an involuntary movement. "Hold still!" she snapped. With that, I lost what little control I had over my emotions and after Miss Cochran left the room, I broke down and cried.

When I finally returned to physical therapy, I continued struggling to overcome my physical limitations. Charlotte came to visit again and saw that I was really trying, but not progressing. At last, in Charlotte's eyes, the reality of my condition was undeniable and for once, she stopped pushing me. She fussed with the staff and finally got a physical therapist to admit that any hope of my being able to walk someday was unrealistic. I was not aware of it, but after this visit Charlotte quit her job and put all of her effort into finding a place where I could concentrate more on education and less on therapy.

CHAPTER 5

A Time to Search

During the summer of 1966, I attended a camp for the handicapped. The program was well designed, and I was grateful that my counselors didn't make me wear my braces very often. Dad arrived at the end of the camp session to drive me home. In the car on the way back to New Jersey we talked about how the summer had gone and then I asked, "When am I going back to Dr. Wright?"

Dad's answer surprised me. "You've gone as far as you can go in those rehabilitation centers," he said. "We're through with them for good. Right now, Charlotte's is trying to get you into a special high school in Jersey City."

I was delighted. There would be no more braces. No more struggles. It was the end of a nightmare. After eighteen years of useless effort, I was more than ready to concentrate on the one part of me that really worked, my mind.

Dad also told me that he had hired someone who would, like Ingrid, take care of me at home. When we arrived at our house in Passaic, Dad wheeled me into the kitchen. I saw two beautiful girls sitting at the table with Charlotte. The girls had that day arrived in the United States from Denmark. Charlotte explained that one girl would live with us and the other girl would live with Charlotte's sister, Flossie. I couldn't resist saying, "Which one do we get?" Dad was visibly embarrassed by the silly way I greeted the girls, but later confided that he had been thinking the same thing. Karen, as it turned out, stayed with us. In addition to taking care of me she did the housework, which was minimal since Gerald, Barney, and Irvene no longer lived at home.

The next week, Dad, Charlotte and I flew to St. Louis for Gerald and Nancy's wedding. It was a reformed Jewish service, attended by a few friends and relatives. The only other wedding I had ever witnessed was my father's marriage to Charlotte, but at that time I had been too young to appreciate the deeper meaning of the ceremony. Nancy was the best thing that ever happened to Gerald. She had a cheerful attitude toward life and an easy way about her that made other people feel at home in her presence. Gerald worked with Dad in the family lumber business, so Nancy's new home would be in New Jersey. This was a long way from her family in Missouri, and I suspect her parents felt more like they were losing a daughter than gaining a son.

We returned home to New Jersey after the wedding and Charlotte wasted no time getting started on me. Before I knew it I had a math tutor. I paid little attention to the lessons, however. The siren song of laziness and passivity once again called out to me, and I was content to sit and listen to music or read something light and entertaining. The apathy and laziness I had cultivated in the institutions was narcotic. I did not know how to fight its power over me. "Get off your ass and get motivated!" Dad said. He had always told me that, but now it became his watchword for me. "Make your choice, Bob," he said. "Work hard and develop yourself or give up and become a vegetable." Those words hurt, yet did not wake me up. I had to be pushed to do things that did not mean very much to me and pushed to do anything that required effort on my part.

The special high school Charlotte wanted me to attend was a day school for the disabled, similar to the Cerebral Palsy Center in Clifton. The A. Harry Moore School was, I think, associated in some way with the Jersey City Teachers College. Charlotte soon discovered that the principal, for some reason, was not interested in me. She put Charlotte off, demanding that a medical doctor see me before she could consider admitting me to the school. Her continual emphasis on my physical condition annoyed Charlotte, who wondered, "Why can't she accept the medical evaluations we already have?" I remember overhearing Charlotte's end of a telephone conversation in which she literally cried with frustration at the principal's excuses for not admitting me. But Charlotte was not the kind of woman who took no for an answer. Somehow she convinced that principal to give me a chance.

I commuted to Jersey City in a station wagon provided by the city bus service. The driver was a Jehovah's Witness. I didn't know what a Jehovah's Witness was, but she seemed to share my religious curiosity. We often talked about God. I accepted the books and the copy of the Jehovah's Witness Bible she gave me, but I didn't read any of them because I was afraid my father or Charlotte would catch me. They kept their distance from religious people and considered religion to be a pointless distraction from the practical concerns of daily life.

I was happy to be living at home again and happy to be in what I thought was a real academic situation. The A. Harry Moore School was not the best, but at least I was doing high school level work. I took beginning French, world history, general science, and English. I tried a math course, but soon dropped it. I had been away from a real classroom for several years, and didn't really know how to study and manage my time. The grades on my first report card were a disappointment, barely passing. But the way Charlotte kept after me—I had no choice but to become educated. At first this was very unpleasant. She spared nothing to make me feel guilty for not studying hard. Her persistence paid off. My second report card showed I had some brains. It was the first positive return on my efforts I had earned in years.

Sometime during that school year, I became very friendly with a handicapped girl my own age. One morning, she and I were riding to school together in the back seat of the station wagon. We started kissing. As luck would have it, the principal was standing at the school entrance. We were caught in the act. She escorted us to her office for a long lecture, shaming us and accusing us of disturbing the driver.

The principal succeeded in humiliating the girl, but I was furious.

I saw no harm in kissing this girl and I resented being scolded like a naughty little boy. When I related the story, my whole family roared with laughter. But it was a long, long time before I could see anything funny about it. Thinking back, I am amazed at the ignorance of some of the people allowed to govern schools for the handicapped. This principal was one of those well-meaning but overprotective people who tend to forget that the handicapped have the same emotional and social needs as everyone else.

In addition to my frustration with the stifling social atmosphere, I began to feel that something else at the school was amiss. I eventually decided the problem was in the quality of the teaching. Here, as in every school I had ever attended, the mentally slow students were put in the same classroom with the physically slow but mentally able. It should have been obvious to any observer that the students weren't slow for the same reasons. Yet placing intelligent, physically disabled students in classrooms where the teaching is watered down to accommodate the slow learners and the mentally retarded was common practice. It was, in my opinion, unreasonable. Thankfully, attitudes about educating the handicapped have changed considerably since the 1960's. Along the way, some community schools voluntarily integrated certain physically disabled students into the regular classes. The Americans with Disabilities Act of 1990 forced the issue and required all schools to accommodate disabled students. I'm not sure, however, that integration is always the best solution, because of the difficulties certain disabilities present. For instance, how can a teacher be fair to a student who is unable to complete the daily amount of work because of a physical handicap? I wish I had a good answer to this problem, but I don't.

Charlotte, aware of the situation I was facing at school, determined to get me into a better environment even if it meant sending me to Europe. Ideas about Europe came from the Danish women who worked for us: first Ingrid, and now Karen. Karen was a loving, good-natured person. Her dependable service as our housekeeper and my caretaker is what made living at home and going to school possible for me. During the time Karen was with us, I went with her to social gatherings at the Danish Seaman's Church in New York City. Everything Dad, Charlotte, and I learned about Denmark from Karen and her friends sounded so interesting that my parents made arrangements for me to go there during the summer. I was to visit Ingrid and then attend a camp for the handicapped. But before the summer came, Karen began spending a lot of time with a guy named Mogens. I suspected that something was going to happen and indeed, before long, Karen became pregnant. When she broke the news to Dad and Charlotte, she was blunt and to the point. She intended to keep the child and to marry Mogens. Karen asked us to attend her wedding, but Dad wanted to do something more for her. He was pleased to act as Karen's father during the ceremony, giving the bride away.

~

Soon after the end of the school year in 1967, I was on the way to Denmark. My flight from New York arrived in Copenhagen forty-five minutes early, so it didn't surprise or concern me that Ingrid wasn't waiting to greet me when I got off the plane. The airline personnel would escort me through customs and stay with me until she arrived. All that mattered to me at that moment was that I was in Denmark at last. I scanned the crowd for Ingrid, expecting her to appear at any moment. But minutes passed, then an hour. She was long overdue.

I couldn't remain at the airport all day, but what choice did I have? Finally an English-speaking woman from the airline took me to the police office. I explained that Ingrid was supposed to meet my plane at nine that morning, and gave the address of some friends of Ingrid's where she said we would be staying. After a couple of hours of telephoning, the police located Ingrid's friends, who came at once.

"Ingrid is still on her way to Copenhagen," they said. "She thinks you are arriving at nine o'clock this evening!" I was too tired to laugh. But it was comical. Ingrid's friends took me to their apartment, fed me and let me rest. At five o'clock that afternoon, Ingrid walked in, unaware that I was already in the apartment and that I could hardly wait to see the dumbfounded look on her face when she saw me sitting there.

I loved Denmark and the Danish people. Ingrid and I toured Copenhagen and visited some of the more famous churches and castles, including Elsinor, where the action of Hamlet takes place. She took me to the Tivoli Music Hall where I heard the young American soprano, Evelyn Lear. I've been to the Tivoli Music Hall many times since, but none of those visits can compare with the thrill I experienced the first time Ingrid took me there.

I was scheduled to attend an international summer camp for handicapped young people. Most of the youths were from Denmark, Sweden, Norway, and Germany. I was the only one from the United States. Language was not a problem, because the workers all understood English. Camp activities were scheduled according to the wishes of the campers. If a group wanted to go swimming in the sea, it was arranged. If some wanted to play games, that too was arranged. I was the only camper in a wheelchair, so the staff had it fairly easy. Ingrid worked at the camp during the last two weeks of the session.

We spent the rest of the summer in Darum, the small town on the west coast of Denmark where Ingrid lived. I met her whole family and her many friends. One of them was Hanne, who returned with me to New Jersey to live with my family. Even though Hanne didn't become pregnant, as Karen did, she, too, met her husband-to-be in America.

I loved Denmark so much, that I ended up spending the next five summers there, staying with families we found by placing advertisements in Danish newspapers.

I knew that Charlotte was trying to find a better school for me, but I was not told until years later of the obstacles she encountered during her search. I suppose it was just as well that I didn't know, because I probably would not have appreciated what she went through. I would have taken her efforts for granted, just as I did everything else.

She began while I was at the D.T. Watson Home in Pittsburgh. Initially, she asked the NYU Rehabilitation Center (where I'd had the evaluation at the Rusk Institute) to give her the names of schools that provided quality education for the handicapped. Each time she asked, they gave her a few names and sent her on her way. It was during my last year at the Home that Charlotte finally quit her job in order to follow up every lead. It seemed that she went on one wild goose chase after another. She made a trip to New Hampshire armed with the names of schools for the handicapped only to discover that enrollment was restricted to the residents of the state. Some of the "schools" she visited in other states didn't even have classrooms. They provided only basic physical care. Eventually she decided that the people at the Rehabilitation Center weren't serious about helping her. They just wanted to get rid of her.

Charlotte also made several trips to Washington, D.C. to meet with Robert Hall at the Department of Health, Education, and Welfare. He gave her the names of a few "schools" and Charlotte explored each one. Some were just hospitals and others only accepted state residents. She pleaded with Mr. Hall for the name of a school. It could be anywhere, she said, anywhere in the world. But none of the places he suggested even came close to what Charlotte wanted for me.

Finally Charlotte arrived for an appointment at Mr. Hall's office only to be told he was at home, ill. "When do you expect him back in the office?" They could not (or would not) say. Even Charlotte had a limit to the amount of frustration she could bear, and suddenly had an attack of hysterics right in front of everyone in the office. One of the secretaries took pity and telephoned Mr. Hall. Charlotte again asked,

"Where can I get information on residential schools for the handicapped? Just tell me which office has this information and I will go there."

"Mrs. Kaplowitz, I understand what you are asking," he said. "But our office has a grant from the government to establish training centers for therapists for the physically handicapped. All our efforts are along those lines."

"Then who can help me find residential schools for the physically handicapped?"

"No one," Hall said. "Mine is the office where that sort of research should be done, but our funds are specifically earmarked for the establishment of training centers for physical therapists. We may not spend that money to locate schools, and I don't know of any other office with that function or with that information."

Finally it was clear to Charlotte. She had reached an impasse in her dealings with the Federal Government. Nevertheless, she continued searching in spite of the overwhelming odds against her. In desperation, Charlotte went to see people who had established small residential boarding homes of their own. Most of them had cerebral palsied children who were mentally retarded and needed companionship. In a few homes, a parent gave the children some elementary education. As nice as some of the homes were, none of them were what Charlotte wanted for me. At home after home, however, one name kept coming up: The Mathany School in Peapack, New Jersey. Charlotte had never once considered visiting the Mathany School. She had heard that all the children were mentally retarded and that the school only went to the eighth grade. I was finishing the ninth. But after hearing his name at so many homes, it occurred to Charlotte that Walter Mathany might be able to help her. She drove over to Peapack and told him everything she had been through and what she was hoping to find. Walter Mathany let her talk. Then he grinned. "I know the very place you're looking for," he said. "The Crippled Children's School."

CHAPTER 6

Faith, Hope and Love

Charlotte was ecstatic. She hurried home, called the Crippled Children's School[3], made airline reservations, and in no time, she and Dad were on the way to Jamestown, North Dakota.

Everything they saw at the Crippled Children's School was a revelation to Dad and Charlotte, but most remarkable was the director, Dr. Anne Carlsen. Dr. Carlsen understood the social and emotional needs of handicapped people very well, because she had been physically disabled from birth. Her arms were short, rounded stumps. She had no legs, yet she walked, even outdoors during North Dakota's harsh winters, using artificial legs and special crutches. Dr. Carlsen had earned a Ph.D. in education and had been a teacher for some years before coming to the Crippled Children's School. Dr. Carlsen did not allow the disability to overshadow the person. As long as a child was able to function mentally, no matter how severe his physical handicap, Dr. Carlsen found a way to help him learn. Under her care I would be treated like an ordinary human being, could finish high school, and, maybe, go on to college.

After admiring Dr. Carlsen's accomplishments, Charlotte said, "Why doesn't anyone back home know about your school? I don't know how many times I asked the NYU Rehab Center for the name of a school like this. Can't you

---

3   In recognition of Dr. Anne Carlsen's many years of service at the Crippled Children's School, the school is now called the Anne Carlson Center.

get a description of your school into their hands? And when I think of the local cerebral palsy centers and those parents who don't know what to do with their children . . . couldn't you post information there? People desperately need to know about your school."

Dr. Carlsen looked at Charlotte intently. "They do know," she said. "I meet either Dr. Rusk or his first assistant at every convention I attend, and we always have a long conversation. They know exactly what our facilities are, what services we provide."

"Then why didn't they tell me? Do you know how many times I've been there? I've begged them for information!"

Dr. Carlsen apparently had heard stories like this before. She said, "Mrs. Kaplowitz, I don't know what to tell you, but I am sure they know everything there is to know about my school. We have been here for many years. They have known about us all along."

Much later in life, when I finally learned what Charlotte had gone through to find the Crippled Children's School I was shocked. And I was profoundly grateful, because finding that school was the turning point in my life.

In spite of my eager anticipation to attend the Crippled Children's School, my first few months did not go smoothly. The main reason for my trouble was a high school teacher named Sharon Bergstrom. Young, ambitious Miss Bergstrom would not tolerate indolence or inferior scholarship simply because her charges had physical handicaps. She expected us to work hard and think hard. In her classroom I faced the toughest academic challenge I had ever encountered. I felt awkward, out of place, and unable to compete. The influence of the other students didn't help matters. It seemed none of them could stand Miss Bergstrom and some actually said they hated her. One student treated her with open contempt because she wouldn't let him have his own way. He refused to compromise and in the end, defeated only himself. He quit school.

This tenor of testing the limits and negative talking made it hard for me to see that under the surface, most of the students respected Miss Bergstrom. They just wouldn't admit it. Miss Bergstrom was tough, but the students who weren't afraid to apply themselves benefited from her discipline for the rest of their lives. In time, I came to understand the truth, but during the beginning weeks of school, I thought I was the victim, not the problem. My perception was that I worked hard in class. In reality, I avoided difficult work by slow, passive behavior, since in the past, someone had either stepped in to take over for me or shortened my assignment. It threw me when Miss Bergstrom stood firm. From my first day at school she expected me to complete all of my work as fast as the other students. When she rejected my obvious attempts to get on her good side, I rebelled at her demands. Several times during my first month of school I stormed out of Miss Bergstrom's classroom in a volcanic blast of rage, shoving my wheelchair backward with my feet, forcing my way out the door and down the hallway. One day my effort to make the most of a head cold prompted Miss Bergstrom to place a note on my typewriter. I quickly scanned the message and saw that she was calling me a hypochondriac. I exploded in a blast of temper and thrust my wheelchair backward out of the classroom with all the strength I had, cursing Miss Bergstrom to her face.

When Charlotte called Dr. Carlsen to check on my progress, she discovered what was going on and went into action. Charlotte called me on the telephone and began scolding like a wet, Jewish mother hen. Exposure to Charlotte's fury could be very motivating, and in no time she had convinced me to re-think my behavior. Charlotte also wrote a letter to Miss Bergstrom, who then became more patient with me. Thankfully, I was old enough to learn quickly from my mistakes, and began to realize that my biggest handicap was my own resistance to hard work. God used Charlotte in my life to help me overcome my laziness and passivity. This was the last time that she would have to berate me for my behavior.

On top of making academic adjustments, I had to learn to get along with the other students. Again, my temper made life more difficult for me. Oddly, I became the good friend of a boy who was also given to emotional eruptions. Norman could not form understandable syllables. To communicate, he spelled out words on his typewriter using a pointer strapped to his forehead. Our friendship was punctuated by sharp disagreements that often turned into temper tantrums. Nevertheless, Norman's intense will to overcome his limitations attracted me and inspired me to push myself to work harder. I never found out why, but after Norman graduated from CCS high school he lost all ambition and retreated into a life of isolation.

The other boys were interested in sports and rock music, so besides being older, I had little in common with them. A day didn't go by when one of the guys I secretly called Big Mouth, Rotten Egg, and The Instigator didn't raise some disturbance in the dorm or the classroom. I tried to stay clear of the troublemakers and usually succeeded. Most of the troubles, all of which the CCS staff handled very well, involved ordinary schoolboy and schoolgirl mischief.

School regulations granted each dorm the choice of staying up late on either Friday or Saturday night. Most of the guys in my dorm thought staying up on Saturday night was a big thing. It seldom mattered to me, but once I wanted to stay up on Friday night to watch a special television program about opera. I couldn't get any cooperation from the guys and was upset, partly because I was in my early twenties and resented the fact that the younger students could overrule me so easily. I appealed to the principal, Edna Cussack. Because Miss Cussack could handle any problem with ease, fairness, and sensitivity, I felt free to talk to her about almost anything.

Though she could not change the policy, Miss Cussack handled my frustration with such diplomacy that I came away from her office neither disappointed nor angry. I never forgot the incident, however, and was surprised many years later to find a mail-order company offering a video recording of the very same show the guys had made me miss. I ordered a copy and got to see the show after all.

~

During the school term, when I was in North Dakota and away from direct contact with my family, I felt free to investigate the Bible and the church. The student body was required to attend chapel every Wednesday morning. I grew curious about church and I started attending an Episcopal Church on Sunday mornings. I liked the liturgy and the general atmosphere, and attending church services also gave me a convenient excuse to get away from the school and go into town. In Sunday school, I delighted in making a show of my copy of the Jewish Old Testament and challenging the Episcopalians with difficult questions. To their credit, the church members overlooked my arrogance and were very kind to me. Although I enjoyed studying the Bible, even studying privately with the minister, I really had no concept of a personal God. My interest in religion and in my Jewish heritage primarily served to boost my pride and give me a sense of identity. I usually behaved as though I were the most important person in the world.

Mercifully, God was not finished with me yet. There were times when I felt overwhelmed and uncertain about my future. I began to wonder if there was anything else to my life besides my education, and I began to rethink my purpose for living. In February of my senior year one of the school secretaries died unexpectedly. The Crippled Children's School was a close-knit community, so losing Evelyn affected everyone. Up until then, I had attached great importance to my academic accomplishments. Evelyn's death made me question whether they had any lasting value.

The school invited Evelyn's pastor to conduct a memorial service during chapel. In his sermon, Walter Trim told us we only had one life to live and that we had better live it for God's glory. I didn't really understand what he meant, but Trim seemed to look right at me when he said, "No man can be good enough to live for God's glory unless he first repents and believes in Jesus Christ!" I couldn't believe the man's arrogance. The idea of not being good enough shot right through my Jewish pride. I rebounded with my usual air of superiority. After all, I was Jewish, and already a very moral and humble person.

One of Evelyn's friends was Doris. I was constantly in and out of Doris' office because she kept the students' spending money. Doris also attended Pastor Trim's church and I knew it. The day after Evelyn's memorial service I went straight to Doris' office and told her just what I thought of her Bible—thumping pastor and his sermon. She patiently let me have my say, but probably felt like beating me over the head for criticizing a sermon that was meant to be a testimony to Evelyn's faith in Christ.

"I don't need Jesus!" I said.

"Just wait and see, Bob," Doris replied. "I think you'll find out for yourself." That's when Doris started praying for me.

Thoughts about the brevity of life troubled me throughout the winter. I was on the verge of grasping the prize I so desperately wanted—my high school diploma—but now, I wondered if the struggle to overcome my disabilities and accomplish something with my life wasn't just meaningless effort. Then, on Wednesday, April 1, Walter Trim spoke at chapel again. He brought the traveling evangelists Ralph and Lou Sutera with him. The Sutera twins told interesting stories about growing up in a rough part of New York City and about how the power of God had enabled Ralph to recover from a fatal illness. Then they preached a gospel sermon and played the violin and vibraphone. Before they left, the Sutera brothers invited everyone to come to the Baptist church on Thursday evening to watch a film about the Vietnam War. I wasn't interested in the war, but I went to the meeting because I wanted to question the brothers about the gospel. As it turned out, when the meeting ended, I didn't have a chance to talk to them.

The next morning I went straight to Doris' office and asked her to tell the Suteras that I wanted to speak to them. Ralph, Lou, and Pastor Trim came the following afternoon. I was a bit excited and a bit afraid because I wasn't sure how to say what I wanted to say. My thoughts were jumbled. I wondered how Doris, though saddened, had responded to Evelyn's death with a positive attitude. I wondered why the Sutera brothers and the people at the Baptist church seemed to have a confidence and security about life that I couldn't understand.

Lou wanted to tour the school and talk to some other students, so I invited Ralph and Pastor Trim into the room where I kept my records and small stereo. I blurted out something about being Jewish, becoming interested in God as a result of my mother's death, and now attending church. Ralph shifted his big Bible in his hands. "Bob," he said, "when the Spirit of God begins to nag someone's conscience, He's telling us we're guilty of breaking God's Law. No man ever lived who could keep all of God's Law, but Christ did. He was perfect. That's why His life could pay the price for your sins and nothing that you do with your life can."

"Jesus' work doesn't end with death on the cross," said Pastor Trim. "He rose from the dead. That shows God's power to give eternal life. No one earns it; it's a gift. But you have to receive it."

"How do I do that?"

"Accept it by faith. Just put your life in Christ's hands," said Ralph.

I hesitated. "Can I . . . be a Jew and a Christian at the same time?"

Ralph opened his Bible to Galatians 3:28-29. "There is neither Jew nor Greek . . . for ye are all one in Christ Jesus. And if ye be Christ's, then are ye Abraham's seed, and heirs according to the promise." I accepted Christ as my Savior without further question. It was not an emotional experience, but I did feel that the heavy weight of hopelessness had lifted from my heart. From that day forward, God was no longer an abstract concept to me. He was real and He cared about what happened to me. According to Ralph and Pastor Trim, I had become a "completed" Jew. Pastor Trim invited me to make a public confession of my faith at the church, which I did that Sunday night. In preparation for my baptism a month later, I studied the Bible with Pastor Trim to be sure I understood the significance of the sacrament.

I was happy about my new faith, yet I knew it would disturb my father. He thought religion was for weak individuals who wanted to escape reality. He had made it very clear that he considered my previous contacts with religious people to be a waste of time. How could I make him understand my new relationship with God? Dad considered himself a self-made man, the master of his fate. After a hitch in the Navy during World War II he purchased a declining lumber company and made it flourish. He trained my brother to be successful in the family business and he spared no expense to keep me from becoming stagnant and unproductive. Gerald and I owe what we are to Dad's compulsive drive, practical mind, and generosity. Because I appreciated everything Dad had ever done for me, I didn't want him to feel hurt or rejected by my decision to accept the Christian faith. On April 6, 1970, I summoned the courage to write:

Dad,

It is difficult for me to say what I am about to, but I must because I am your son and you are my father. Something wonderful has happened in my life. I have sincerely accepted the Christian faith. If you ask me how, I can tell you, but I cannot tell you why except that this is something I have wanted for quite a long time. I have never been so happy in my life. Accepting the Christian faith was my own decision. The school had nothing to do with it.

I do not know what your reaction will be, but you cannot stop me for I have already accepted the Lord Jesus Christ in my heart. I still love my family, and now I shall love you even more. Do not be angry with me for I believe what I did was right and I am old enough to make my own decisions in life.

I hope I have not shocked you too much, but if I have, I am sorry. Call me. This has been the most difficult letter in my life to write to you.

Your loving son,
Bob

I was apprehensive about receiving Dad's call, so Doris offered to be on hand to explain any details that my father might want to know concerning the Christian faith. As soon as he finished reading my letter, Dad dialed my number. I went to Doris' office to receive the call, and when she switched on the speakerphone, Dad said, "Son, are you there?" The word "son" told me all I needed to know. I cried with relief, and Dad told me that he still loved me. He said he only wanted to be sure my decision made me happy. In parting, Dad reminded me not to let religious activities interfere with my education.

Right away everyone at school heard about my conversion. As a result, during the week following I overheard a scrap of conversation that taught me an important lesson about God. Bernice, who worked at the school and attended Pastor Trim's Church, and Mrs. Publow, the mother of a student, were telling Agnes Austin, one of the teachers, something about me. I didn't figure out what they were saying because they changed the subject when they noticed I was listening. Later Bernice came to me and explained.

She and Mrs. Publow had been praying for me for a long time. When they learned that I had surrendered my life to Jesus Christ, they had been deeply moved by the answer to prayer. That's what they had been telling Agnes Austin. Then Bernice told me something else. Mrs. Publow was not well. Besides struggling to care for her handicapped daughter, Mrs. Publow struggled with leukemia. I was shocked. The same thing had happened to my mother, except that it had happened so fast that Mother never knew she was going to die. How could Mrs. Publow stand it? How could she seem so confident and secure? "She trusts God to take care of all her problems," Bernice said. "She believes that God has a purpose in everything that happens." It wasn't hard for me to imagine God having a purpose in good things, but I wondered how He could have a purpose in bad things. Then I remembered Jesus' prayer the night he was betrayed, "Father, all things are possible unto thee. Take away this cup from me; Nevertheless, not what I will, but what thou wilt." Jesus' death was a terrible thing, yet God had something good in mind when He allowed it to happen. It didn't matter whether or not I understood God's purpose in leukemia or cerebral palsy, I reasoned. I had only to accept the difficulties set before me, as Jesus accepted the task set before him, and leave the outcome in God's hands.

Without realizing she had done so, Mrs. Publow taught me a lesson about the sovereignty of God that spared me much confusion and bitterness in later years. Because of her example of courage and faith, I settled in my mind at the beginning of my Christian life that God had an ultimate purpose for me. That made the severity of my handicap and everything that had happened to me because of it easier to accept.

I never saw Ralph and Lou Sutera again, though I corresponded with them for many years. During the last months of school, the people at the First Baptist Church became like a family to me and I studied the Bible with Pastor Trim and the youth director, Lee Johnson. I had studied the Bible before, but this time I expected it to make a difference in my life. I also found it amusing that Walter Trim, a man whom I had criticized severely, had now become an important part of my life.

Another surprising change of heart came over me. Someone I had despised became very dear to me. It was Sharon Bergstrom, the teacher I had blamed when my life at the Crippled Children's School did not begin smoothly. I had been glad when finally she had been asked to leave her teaching position, but I was puzzled when she kept coming back to visit the students as a friend. Perhaps, I thought, Miss

Bergstrom was not as bad as I wanted her to be. My whole outlook on life, it seemed, was changing. I had resented Miss Bergstrom fiercely, but now I began to recognize the many ways she had helped me. Her candor had exposed my faults and taught me to accept honest criticism constructively. Her fortitude had overpowered my tantrums and had taught me the wisdom of presenting my case logically. Finally, she helped me to snap me out of the bondage of passivity. Instead of meeting new challenges with fear, I began to rely on God for my direction. And that, ultimately, is what freed me to explore my intellectual potential.

My time at the Crippled Children's School came to an end in June of 1970, only three months after I had become a Christian. My graduating class consisted of four girls and myself. Toward the end of the year, the five of us took a trip to the North Dakota Bad Lands. We were all handicapped, of course, and accustomed to the fact that, in those days, handicapped accessible public restrooms were seldom available. Along the way we stopped at a picnic area and while the girls and I waited, our chaperones went on a hike to stretch their legs. They must have walked farther than expected, because before they returned the girls and I all felt the need to use the bathroom. Since the picnic area was deserted, the girls simply aimed my wheelchair in a direction that insured their privacy and relieved themselves. But I was at the girls' mercy. I tried valiantly to hold out until our male chaperone returned to assist me, but finally reached the point when I either had to use "the Oscar" (our euphemism for urinal) or wet my pants. The girls were good sports about it, and twenty-five years later, Yvonne still laughs when she remembers Pam saying, "I'll hold the urinal, but I won't touch anything!"

On graduation day, I was twenty-two years old. I was proud of my high school diploma and confident that given the proper amount of time and the right people to help me, I could handle college. Sadly, some students at the school did not care what they did after graduation. It had always been difficult for me to say good-bye, and leaving the Crippled

Children's School for the last time was especially painful. During my three years there, I had become emotionally attached to the staff and students. They had given me faith, hope, and love. And they had changed the course of my life.

CHAPTER 7

My Declaration of Independence

I continued to travel to Denmark during the summers while I was enrolled in the Crippled Children's School. I spent the summer of 1968, after my first year at the school, with Kay, a grade school teacher in his mid-thirties. Kay had been a sailor and spoke passable English. Greta, his wife, was much older than he was and had been married before. It was an unusual relationship, but I didn't think too much about it because I was having such a grand summer partying with their friends. After having lived in the structured environment of institutions for so many years, I found Kay and Greta's free and easy ways liberating. They were not particularly ambitious people and seemed to have plenty of time to spend touring Denmark near Copenhagen with me.

When I returned to Denmark in the summer of 1969, I stayed with Kay and Greta again during the first half of the summer. As usual, there were quite a few parties at their home and at the homes of their friends. When the Danes throw a party, it sometimes lasts for more than a day. Needless to say, some of the things I witnessed were quite racy. At one of these prolonged parties I drank too much gin and soda. After becoming extremely drunk, I was sick to my stomach for twenty-four hours. The horrible consequences of excess convinced me to discipline myself and to take more responsibility for my behavior. When mid-summer came, I was reluctant to leave Kay and Greta. Though I was twenty-one years old, I wept openly when they said good-by.

I was worried about how the rest of my summer in Denmark would turn out. My main fear was that Inger Kehlet, the woman with whom I was to stay, would not be able to communicate with me. Inger spoke no English and I spoke very little Danish. The Kehlet family lived in Bjaert, a two—hour drive from Ingrid's home. The moment I saw it, I fell in love with the Kehlets' old farmhouse. It had the look of a cottage one might find pictured in a fairy tale book and Bjaert the look of a fairy tale village. The Kehlets seemed friendly enough, but I felt lost living with a family that spoke no English. I settled in my mind to do whatever I could to help the situation and made an effort to understand and speak as much Danish as possible. Still, it was awkward and I was grateful when soon after my arrival at the Kehlets', Ingrid took me to her house for a weekend and gave me some insight on how to adjust to my new surroundings.

Inger Kehlet turned out to be a wonderful woman with a sense of humor and a warm, loving heart. She was always doing kind things for people in the town and constantly welcoming people into her home. Inger's husband owned a livestock operation, trading pigs and cattle. From what I could understand, he was a smart businessman. Inger's son, who gradually showed himself to be a practical joker, was quiet and reserved like his father, but Inger did enough talking for all three.

Inger was sensitive enough to realize that I wanted to make myself understood no matter how long it took. She waited patiently as I searched a small dictionary for the Danish words I needed to say. I listened for Danish words that were used often and tried to use them in context on my own. To my surprise, most of the time I was understood. Inger made breaking the language barrier easy for me through her natural ability to pantomime. All her friends thought she was marvelously funny. Inger knew it, and it kept her going. Fortunately, one of her son's friends, Sven Rorbaek, spoke English and translated the important things Inger and I needed to communicate to each other. Sven Rorbaek's family took an interest in me and invited me to accompany them to their summer cottage beside a lake in the middle of Jutland. I remember that sunsets reflecting on the surface of this lake were indescribably beautiful.

When I returned to Inger Kehlet's home in Bjaert, Denmark, to spend the summer of 1970, I was a new man in Christ. Inger saw that I was reading the Bible and she was glad. She, too, was a Christian. She told me she believed God helped her take care of me. I am convinced she was right. Between the language barrier and the amount of physical attention I required, the two of us often wondered how we ever managed.

Early that summer, Ingrid came to Bjaert to tell me something. She was going to be married. This news came as a shock, because I had never considered the possibility that Ingrid might marry. In fact, I secretly wanted to marry her myself. Ingrid said she had delayed her wedding until the summer just so I could attend. The man she was to marry, a Lutheran pastor, was much older than she. His wife had been ill for many years, and it was Ingrid who had taken care of her until she died. He had a number of children, all married, and quite a few grandchildren. During World War II, this man had risked his life to save Danish Jews from Nazi exterminators.

When I had time to sort out my emotions, I felt truly happy for Ingrid and looked forward to the wedding and festivities. I wanted my wedding present to her to be something special. I remembered Ingrid's admiration of a beautiful tablecloth at the Kehlets', so I asked Inger to find one like it for me to give to Ingrid. In addition, I presented Ingrid with a painting I had done at the Crippled Children's School. Unlike "my" watercolor that President Kennedy's Committee for the Handicapped had awarded years earlier, the painting Ingrid received was a genuine Kaplowitz—an abstract landscape.

Ingrid was married in one of the oldest churches in Denmark, a small structure dating back to the 11th century. The church was crowded with people. I couldn't understand all of the Danish, but it didn't matter. The fact that two people were being united in love was evident enough. The dinner that followed the ceremony lasted into the wee hours.

I felt privileged to witness one of the happiest moments in Ingrid's life.

The freedom and acceptance I experienced in Danish society strongly influenced my determination not to live the rest of my life in an institution. I launched my college career immediately after returning from Bjaert in August of 1970. The Crippled Children's School staff had encouraged me to go to college after high school. Upon their recommendation I, and three of the four girls in my graduating class, had applied to Lake Region Junior College, a small school with wheelchair accessible facilities about an hour and a half drive north of Jamestown. I was naive about many aspects of living independently, but had confidence in my ability to succeed. I also hoped that remaining in North Dakota near my friends in Jamestown would make it easier for me to continue growing in my new Christian faith. As it turned out, I was on the verge of making a lonely journey through my own private circles of hell. It was just a coincidence, but the town was called Devil's Lake.

In order for me to live independently outside of an institution, I had to hire a roommate. This person would have to bathe and dress me, feed me and brush my teeth, take me to class, and do almost everything but think for me. It was a tall order. Dad and I were very apprehensive about the situation, and we discussed the matter with the college dean before school started. With his help, we located and hired my first roommate, Konrad.

Konrad had a family, but his wife and child remained in their hometown while he attended classes in Devil's Lake. Konrad was interested only in the financial benefits my father and I promised, and saw only to the essentials of my care. His generally insolent and insensitive behavior created a lot of tension between us. One time, however, Konrad took me with him on a weekend trip to his home. When I saw what a callous husband and father he was, I stopped blaming myself for the problems we were having.

Regardless of my trouble with Konrad, I was still a student at Lake Region and had to take classes. Because

I had some writing ability, I decided that English would be the most practical thing for me to study. I took all of the literature and drama courses offered at Lake Region. I discovered that two of the professors who taught those courses were opera buffs. One taught opera appreciation. I took the class and received the highest grade without studying. I breezed through music appreciation the same way, except that my grade was not as high. That professor gave more assignments, and I had difficulty completing them on time. Most of the students thought these two professors were difficult and demanding. I think, rather, that the students just weren't familiar with the subject matter, because I never had a problem. For me, opera and music appreciation were a refreshing change from the required courses.

None of the classes were paced for a physically handicapped student, and keeping up with the assignments was a constant struggle for me. In order to graduate, I had to take courses in which I had no interest. Biology and "Physical Education for Men," for example, held no interest for me. Improving my study habits helped to bring my grades up a little, but in the end, I had to accept the limitations my handicap imposed. I simply did my best and lived with the results.

My struggle to compete academically was not my greatest difficulty at Lake Region. I had lived a sheltered life, surrounded by people who understood and accommodated my handicap. The independence I had experienced in Bjaert, Denmark, where I was considered a part of the community, had led me to the mistaken assumption that everyone at Lake Region Junior College would likewise accept me. In reality, I was emotionally unprepared to live in a society that was openly indifferent to and uncomfortable with the presence of a severely handicapped person. I felt hurt and confused when few people at school showed any interest in me. I think my speech difficulty was one reason my classmates felt intimidated by me. Those who did acknowledge my presence either spoke over me as if I was deaf, or spoke to me through someone else as if I needed an interpreter to understand plain English. They also seemed embarrassed to ask me to repeat myself if they couldn't understand me the first time. Nevertheless, even if I had been able to speak clearly, I could add little to the talk about sports and girls that dominated the conversation of the other guys. My interests, classical music and opera, were out of place. With dismay, I remembered Norman, my explosive but determined friend from the Crippled Children's School. Was social rejection what drove him to give up on life and retreat into isolation? I didn't want that to happen to me. I enjoyed living and being with other people.

Fortunately, I had some encouragement from the two professors who shared my love of music. Because they chatted with me from time to time about some aspect of music or about my reaction to a particular performer or composition, I didn't feel like such an opera-loving oddball. Their friendliness made it a little easier for me to go through this whole unhappy experience, but they were often too busy to really listen to me or to help me with my problems. Loneliness, Konrad's indifference, and the effort it took to make passing grades often discouraged me beyond what I thought I could bear. I began to experience periods of depression.

John Anthony, my psychology professor at Lake Region, came to my rescue again and again, encouraging me to keep up my spirits and to keep trying. John also went out of his way to encourage other handicapped students, three of whom were the girls who had graduated with me from the Crippled Children's School. The girls and I had gone our separate ways at Lake Region, and they had no idea that I was going through such difficult times. Their physical disabilities were not as severe as my own and they could easily melt into the community. I seemed to float on top.

I came very close to giving up, and probably would have, had it not been for the people at a small Baptist church. Pastor Lee Borders reached out to me with friendship and renewed my determination to push on. Occasionally, an older couple from the church invited me to their farm for a weekend. Those times away from the town, my roommate, and my classes provided more emotional relief than I realized at the time. Apart from the graciousness of God, I don't know where I found the courage and strength to continue. Incredible as it sounds, it never dawned on me that I could ask God to supply my needs.

I began to understand, however, that the appreciation of fine music was a gift God had given me. Listening to the records I played on my small stereo helped develop my mind and protect it from harm. Absorbing myself deeply in a piece of music was not an addiction or an escape from reality. It was the only way I knew to relieve the great stress I was under. I was physically helpless—I couldn't even go for a walk by myself. Music was my outlet. I listened actively, concentrating on the patterns and the message of the sounds I heard. Through this participation in music, my spirit was refreshed.

Toward the end of the first year I met Wayne, a student nearing graduation. He became my first friend. Wayne enjoyed my company and I came to trust him. He fed me, took me places, and did things to help me but never accepted payment. Konrad resented this interference, but I didn't care. I liked having friends and fun. Wayne took me to his hometown one time, and I saw from the gentle manners and conversation among the members of his devout Catholic family why he had grown up to be such a nice person. When Wayne graduated and moved on I felt like I'd lost my best friend. But I did have one satisfaction. While under my influence, Wayne had developed a taste for opera.

My roommate the second year turned out to be epileptic. Early in the semester he began drinking heavily and his condition grew worse. Distraction and worry tormented me, because my daily sustenance depended on this undependable man. I did not know how to deal with the problem, but soon it took care of itself. He dropped out of school and I found another roommate. John was the replacement, and he turned out to be very reliable, but he was mentally slow. He became a valued friend who willingly and faithfully helped me, even taking me to visit my friends at the Crippled Children's School when he went to his parents' home near Jamestown. Owing to John's dependable and pleasant nature, the momentary mishaps that were a way of life with him didn't upset me. However, I generally was at a loss when faced with major difficulties. I depended on Pastor Borders to resolve those for me.

Sadly, Devil's Lake did not turn out, as I'd hoped, to be a good place for me to grow in the Christian faith. The only Christian friends I found were the people at the Baptist church. These people were very gracious to me, but did not know how to disciple me. They focused mainly on evangelism and on their ministry at a nearby Indian reservation. There were no Christian ministries or Bible studies on campus that I knew of and no other students who seemed interested in developing their faith in God. I didn't know where to look for help. I didn't even know what kind of help I needed.

I was nearing the end of my second year when psychology professor John Anthony suggested I might be happier at the University of North Dakota at Grand Forks. I was open to suggestions, but unsure that I could handle the work at a university. John recommended that I take a course at the Grand Forks campus during the summer. Then I would find out for myself whether or not I could make the grade. Taking a summer course meant an end to my summers in Denmark, but I recognized that I was at a crossroads. I could not spend every summer abroad if I wanted to further my college education. Also, I knew I needed to do something or go somewhere that would help me grow in the Christian faith.

Up until then, I had never planned anything without first consulting my parents. Now, at age twenty-four, without asking Dad and Charlotte's advice, I made the first major decision of my life. I registered for the course.

CHAPTER 8

My Heart's Desire

I took just one course at the University of North Dakota during the summer of 1973, an introduction to Shakespeare. I was under pressure to succeed, because how well I did in the course would determine my future, if any, at the university.

I had to rely on UND's Handicapped Services to provide my roommate. They found one for me, but very soon, to my displeasure, he started smoking marijuana in our room. When I protested, he said, "If you tell anybody about what I do, I'll see to it that you don't have any friends on this campus." After having spent two lonely years at Lake Region, I truly feared what this guy could do to me. Furthermore, his life focused around sex, and he was proud of it. When his girlfriend came to visit, they showed no consideration for my presence, carrying on and copulating as if they enjoyed seeing how much teasing I could take. Lust tempts me as strongly as it tempts any man, since cerebral palsy affects only my body and brain, not my mind. At first I was offended. I felt he was violating not only the girl, but also my Christian morals. I was afraid to stand up for myself, however, and soon I was caught up in my roommate's way of life, even going so far as to attend a bawdy night club to watch the strip tease show. There were times that summer when I firmly believe that, because I had no physical ability to carry out my desires, God protected me from suffering some of the serious consequences of sexual sin. I knew that I was involved in wrongdoing, but I was too weak and dependent to stand up for what I knew to be right. I allowed myself to be controlled by my roommate and by my own strong temptation. Unlike my roommate, though, I did not wholly give myself over to the pursuit of lust. I could only go so far before I found myself turning to God. At first this was of necessity, because I was physically helpless to find healthy ways to blow off the steam of sexual temptation and frustration. Later, I turned to Him of my own choosing; I not only had to do what was morally right, I wanted to.

Somehow, through the grace of God and by attending services at a small Baptist church, I managed to keep my sanity. I was grateful for the Christian fellowship, but unfortunately, like the church in Devil's Lake, this church seemed to be stuck on teaching evangelism. I needed to be taught how God could help me with my problems, especially with my hopeless roommate situation.

On top of the stress I felt over my roommate trouble, I was desperately afraid of failing Introduction to Shakespeare. The course required a lot of reading and written homework, and I could barely keep pace with the syllabus. As I fell further behind with every assignment, I could see my chance of attending the university in the fall diminishing. I worried myself into such an anxious state that I required daily physical therapy to relieve muscle spasms in my back. Now, when I recall that summer, I can't imagine how I coped with all the physical pain and emotional stress.

During the final days of Introduction to Shakespeare, my instructor kindly modified the course requirements and let me pass with just one paper and two oral exams. My paper analyzed and compared Othello in both its Shakespeare and Verdi incarnations. Opera was my intellectual passion. The study of Shakespeare's plays and Verdi's operas had captured my imagination when I was a teenager. I related whatever I was studying to some aspect of opera. That made me appear even more eccentric, but this instructor realized that I was serious about my studies, which is, I suppose, one reason why he passed me.

At the summer's end, I explained my roommate problem to the Director of Handicapped Services. He was dumbfounded. "If I had only known what was going on," he said, "I could have helped you." He promised to get me a more responsible roommate for the next semester, and I promised myself not to be such a pushover.

At first, my new roommate seemed to enjoy my company as much as I enjoyed his. He was a nursing student, and gave me very good physical care. But before long I realized he was unhappy. I was too wrapped up in myself and in my classes to give a thought to my roommate's needs. I took his service to me for granted. When I finally woke up to the fact that something was wrong, I didn't know what it was or what to do about it. Help came a few weeks later. I discovered that some of the guys who lived in the dorm were involved with a Christian group called the Navigators. Mark and Rochey took an interest in me, not just because I was handicapped, but because they were concerned about my spiritual development. I professed to be a Christian, but I was arrogant and worldly. Although I realized that I desperately needed Christian friends, I didn't know how to pray about what I needed.

But I knew something special was happening to me when Mark asked my roommate if he could take care of me for an evening. I was touched by Mark's kindness. It was a rare thing for anyone to volunteer to help me without expecting payment in return. That evening I told Mark how I'd come to North Dakota, how I'd become a Christian, and about the problems I'd had during the summer semester. He offered to help me learn to study the Bible and invited me to a fellowship meeting. He even offered to take me there. The short Bible studies with Mark helped my Christian walk take on a deeper meaning but didn't solve my immediate problems. As the weeks went by, my roommate's discontent became more noticeable. Mark suggested that the job of taking care of me was too big for one person, and advised me to start asking other people to help out. That way, I could give my roommate a little time to himself and it might relieve some of the friction that had built up between us. Rochey was the one who really made the plan work. Through him, I met many guys who were willing to help me.

This arrangement seemed to make things better, but for some reason I was still dissatisfied. One evening after a fellowship meeting I told Mark how I felt. He showed me Philippians 4:6-7, "Be anxious for nothing, but in everything by prayer and supplication with thanksgiving let your requests be made known to God. And the peace of God, which surpasses all comprehension, will guard your hearts and your minds in Christ Jesus." Mark gently pointed out two things. First, I worried too much. In being anxious about everything, I was not turning to God, believing that He could work through my problems. Second, I needed to be more thankful. I had been taking people for granted. Deep in my heart I knew Mark was right, though I was reluctant to admit it. It wounded my pride. But as we talked and prayed together, I confessed my sins in earnest. This was a real breakthrough in my Christian life, the first time since I had become a Christian that I had been honest with God about myself.

I began telling my roommate how much I liked him and appreciated his help. He seemed apathetic towards any kindness I showed him, but I did not allow myself to become angered by his rejection as I might have done in the past. I made the best of the situation and tried to learn as much as possible from my new Christian friends. I was discovering the reality of Proverbs 3:5-6, "Trust in the LORD with all your heart And do not lean on your own understanding. In all your ways acknowledge Him, And He will make your paths straight."

The growth I was experiencing as a result of the Navigator fellowship made me realize I needed to find a different church. Though I enjoyed the people at the small Baptist church I attended, I knew the preaching would always emphasize evangelism rather than discipleship. In my opinion, this emphasis kept believers from maturing. The pastor's wife had shown a lot of interest in me, even writing an article about me for a small Christian publication. This made my leaving the church awkward. Just when I was ready to break the news, the pastor and his family transferred to a church in another state. This was obviously God's timing. Without hurting any feelings, I made the move to Faith Evangelical Free Church where many of my university friends worshipped.

I still had a lot to learn about managing the business of university life in a way that allowed me to make steady academic progress. I started the fall semester with Elizabethan drama, creative writing, and sociology. The demands of three classes quickly overwhelmed me, so I dropped the sociology course. I did not mind working on my degree by taking only one or two courses at a time, because I was learning that I turned into a nervous wreck when I took on too much. Since pressure to meet deadlines sent me into a panic, I tried prioritizing my assignments. To satisfy the requirements of the writing course, I re-wrote and handed in two short stories I had written earlier. This gave me more time to devote to the drama course. Gradually I learned that the best way for someone struggling with disabilities like mine to survive in the educational system was through a combination of independent study and classroom participation. I was by no means the first or the last handicapped student to attend the University of North Dakota. In fact, other students from the Crippled Children's School in Jamestown had continued their education there, and quite a few had succeeded. Some of the classrooms were not accessible to wheelchairs, but the university made every effort to accommodate me. When a class I needed was scheduled in an inaccessible classroom, as was the case with some of my English classes, it was moved to a better location. If a lecture could not be re-located, someone made arrangements for me to be carried up a flight of stairs.

I didn't give my family the details about all the trouble I was having. Whenever I went home they teased me about being a professional student and about being a Christian. They didn't mean any harm—trading wisecracks is the Kaplowitz way. But they all noticed I was becoming a more secure person. When my father came to visit me he was impressed by how willingly my Christian friends took care of me and counted me as part of the group.

When the semester ended in December of 1973, I was triumphant. I had done well with my courses and had found a group of Christian friends who accepted me and helped me. The happiest day came when one of them offered to be my roommate for the coming semester. His name was Harold.

Having Harold for a roommate didn't eliminate the difficulties involved with caring for me. It just made them easier to face. We both tried to live by Christian principles and though I still had a lot to learn, Harold was a good teacher. He was a vocational education major and a guy who always had to be doing something with his hands. He started all sorts of projects but rarely finished any of them. His tinkering and poor use of time made it hard for me to concentrate on my homework when he was in the room, but instead of becoming angry, I forced myself to block out the distractions. In addition to his little projects, Harold was forever fixing up his truck, a dilapidated delivery van. After having had so many difficult roommates, I felt fortunate that Harold's van was his only vice. From that time on, I made up my mind to trust God to provide the right men to take care of me.

At the end of the spring semester of 1974, Mark invited our whole Navigator group to his wedding. We all made the journey, guys and girls, in Harold's van, which he then was in the process of converting into a camper. I'm amazed that we made it to California in time for the wedding. More than once Harold's old beat up truck broke down. We left North Dakota a week early in order to visit places like Mt. Rushmore and Yellowstone Park along the way, but every time we stopped at one of these wonderful places Harold found something on the truck that needed to be repaired. While Harold's head was under the hood, I went sightseeing with the rest of the group.

This trip was in dramatic contrast to the only other long road trip I had ever taken. That was the time my family drove from New Jersey to Florida with Aunt Ida and Uncle Morris before the days of automobile air conditioning. Believe me, it was a miserable drive. Morris was a hypochondriac and I was a whiney little boy about six or seven years old. Between my demands for attention and the complaints of Uncle Morris, by the time that we reached our destination everyone's nerves were ready to snap.

But my group of Navigator friends got along so well together that I felt privileged to be traveling with them. Throughout the week we had devotionals and prayer times and behaved like brothers and sisters. We even took Harold's idiosyncrasies in stride. As we approached San Francisco, Harold decided to put a window in the roof of the camper. As one of the guys drove, Harold grabbed his tools, climbed on top, and started cutting the hole! This was at night. Otherwise the sight of the hippie-style camper with Harold sawing away on top might have stopped the traffic. We crossed a bridge and I was just catching my first glimpse of San Francisco when suddenly the "window" opened. Above me was Harold, poking his head through the hole, obviously satisfied with his version of a job well done.

I met Mark's fiancée, Alice, at a wonderful salmon cookout. She was a sweet Christian and just perfect for Mark. As I observed the love between them, I thought about God's grace and how He works out His plan in each person's life, married or single. I didn't have a girlfriend then, but I hoped that I would be able to find one and to marry someday.

The day after the wedding I flew back to New Jersey. This turned out to be very fortunate for me, because on the return trip to North Dakota a tire on Harold's camper blew out. The guy who told me about the wreck said he turned white with fear. I turned white, just imagining those terrifying moments in that out of control camper. No one was hurt, but it shook me up, thinking about injuries, especially injuries that might make my disability worse.

The trip to California gave me tremendous feelings of confidence and independence. This was partly because my parents did not plan the trip for me and partly because on the road, there were no schedules or comfortable routines or mother hens to control my life. I was surprised to find out that I really did need regular nourishment, a good night's sleep, and sometimes, a nap. I didn't realize how important my routines were until it was up to me to establish them for myself. I also saw how much my independence depended on the friendship and help of other people. I truly appreciated my friends, who wanted me, cared for me, and respected me, simply for who I was.

Although I was happy at the University of North Dakota, my studies were not satisfying to me. Opera was my love and found its way into all of my writings, but instead of pursuing that interest, I stuck to the required courses for an English major. For some reason, I didn't think a person with my handicap could major in music. Above all else, I wanted a college degree. I had to have it. Charlotte, like a typical Jewish mother, was always hounding me and pushing me to do my best and to be the best. With each semester, I inched closer to my goal of a college degree, but my resolve was weakening. Though my heart wasn't in my work, I kept telling myself it was.

The required courses for an English major included two semesters of a foreign language. I decided to tackle German because it would be useful if I went back to Europe. I began the first semester of the language armed with confidence from my success with high school French and the little Danish I spoke. Soon I was in Deutsch up to my neck! I seemed to be studying German all day long just to keep up with the class. Fortunately, a friend tutored me on the side and I managed to survive. In spite of my palsy-related speech difficulties and New Jersey accent, I pronounced German words better than most of my classmates. Perhaps I had developed an ear for Germanic sounds in Denmark. Anyway, because my spoken English is often difficult to recognize, I made a great effort to be understood in German. This actually improved the clarity of my English.

While struggling with German, I took a writing course under the direction of the kind professor who had taught

Introduction to Shakespeare my first summer at UND. Although my studies centered on poetry, literature, and drama, the professor in this independent study allowed me write about opera. My analyses were weak, but at least I was learning to write good papers and I was free to follow my heart. Nevertheless, overall I was losing interest in my studies and it eventually got me into trouble.

One semester I simply left my course registration up to someone in the Handicapped Services office. The course I wanted to take was full, so the person chose what he thought was the next best thing: Elizabethan drama. The books for the course looked familiar, but I kept finding other things to do and never opened them. By the time I caught on to what had happened it was too late to drop the course without a penalty. I couldn't believe it. I was stuck in the very same Elizabethan drama course I had taken a year earlier under a different instructor. I wish I had dropped the course right then and taken the penalty, because it turned into a nightmare. The instructor was an unreasonable wretch, hard to hear, and full of abstract literary jargon.

The trouble was partly my fault. One day I thought I heard the instructor say she would give one test and that would be the end of the course. This sounded odd but agreeable since I was ready to quit anyway. I took the test and never returned to class. A few weeks later I ran into the instructor and she asked where I had been. She was astounded because I thought the course was finished. I was annoyed because she had not been clear. Reluctantly, I agreed to write some kind of paper to satisfy the course requirements. She didn't really say what kind of paper, so I copied information from a few books and gave her what amounted to a report. She refused to accept it. She was again vague about what I was supposed to hand in. After she rejected my second attempt, I withdrew from the class. I had the idea she was harassing me and I didn't have to put up with that. I had earned a decent grade in Elizabethan drama the first time I had taken it!

But I was confused about the episode, wondering if it had really been a learning experience or just a waste of time. Should I have tried to finish the course and do my best (the voice of Charlotte), or was I right to quit in disgust? My conscience bothered me until I met another handicapped student who told me this same woman had placed similar confusing demands on him. When I heard his story, I felt better about my choice.

The following semester I personally signed up for survey of English literature and fine arts symposium. I began the semester feeling emotionally drained after my clash with the drama instructor. My survey of English literature course had three long lectures a week and a long list of required reading. In spite of my intention to do well, I felt disheartened as I surveyed the dismal swamp of literature before me. To cheer me up, my friends invited me to join them on a weekend camping trip. I had never slept outside in a sleeping bag and tent before and was as excited as a kid the whole weekend. We had a few Bible studies and lots of laughs and I caught a cold, but on Monday morning I felt ready to survey English literature again.

By the end of the week I had a bad sore throat and a fever. My head ached. I could barely concentrate during my first exam in English literature, and I failed miserably. Devastated, I dropped the course, and I dropped my English major. Charlotte, and everyone else, would just have to accept my decision. It was final. There was just one loose end I needed to tie up.

A few days before I flunked out of the English department, I attended a fine arts symposium lecture. The subject was opera and choral music. The speaker sounded like a man after my own heart, so I made an appointment with him for one day during the next week to discuss opera. The way things turned out, I went to the interview depressed, exhausted, and resigned to failure. As we talked, a thought flashed through my mind: Would it be possible to graduate from the University of North Dakota with a degree in music literature? To my surprise, this professor offered to design a program especially for me. When I left his office my head was reeling—but not because I now had the chance to study music literature. I had a very high fever. My cold had progressed into pneumonia complicated by infectious mononucleosis. I spent a week in the hospital before I was ready to chart my new course.

I was assigned a new academic advisor, David Stocker. Dave was the first person I had encountered who was genuinely interested in helping me get what I wanted out of a college education. It had taken me years to figure out what seemed so obvious to Dave. I belonged in a music department, not an English department.

When I changed my major from English to music, I broke loose from studies I had been forcing myself to do. My rebellious attitude melted away. I realized that I had convinced myself that I couldn't handle—or perhaps didn't deserve—the challenge of a music major because I couldn't sing or play an instrument. I had been afraid to follow the strong desire God had placed in my heart. Once again I found that my greatest handicap was my own misguided thinking. When I focused on my weaknesses, I could not develop my strengths.

The music department was a refreshing change from the cold arrogance I had encountered in the English department. Even the students were more polite to me. I felt very much at home in my new field of study: operatic music literature. I began with basic music theory, music literature, and an independent study of three nineteenth-century Italian operas. Nineteenth-century Italian opera, the opera of Giuseppe Verdi, was my absolute favorite. No longer did opera whisper to me from the wings. It was at the center of my academic stage and the curtain was going up.

It's a good thing I was thrilled with my independent study course, because music theory was formidable. Learning theory without playing an instrument was somewhat like learning to sing without a voice—academic. Yet with the little finger on my left hand I pressed the keys on my electric organ and trained my ear to recognize steps and half steps, intervals and chords. It was hard and frustrating at times, but I was finally doing something I completely enjoyed. That made the struggle worthwhile.

As the spring semester of 1975 came to an end, it occurred to me that my unhappiness, my illness, and my failure were part of a series of events that I could only understand in retrospect. While the events had occurred, I had been so miserable that I thought God had forgotten me. He was actually answering my prayer that I would grow in the Christian faith. He did this by working out His plan for my life in a way that would teach me to depend on Him. The realization that God might answer prayer in unexpected ways renewed my confidence that God, not I, was in control of my life.

And going into that summer I really needed a strong faith, for I was scheduled to undergo an operation conducted by the most innovative and controversial brain surgeon in the world.

CHAPTER 9

The Brain Stimulator

My parents were far too practical to chase after quack cures for cerebral palsy, but they did explore legitimate medical options. Though brain surgery is quite sophisticated today, it is still dangerous. It was even more risky in the early 1950s, when my parents first learned about the results of Dr. Irving S. Cooper's surgical remedies for involuntary movement disorders.

Almost any movement disorder is referred to as palsy. Shaking palsy, for example, is another name for Parkinson's disease. When Dr. Cooper began treating victims of Parkinson's disease in the late 1940s, he was taught a surgical procedure that stopped the uncontrollable trembling by cutting a nerve pathway in the brain. Like cutting a communications line, this operation stopped the brain messages that were causing the involuntary movements. This surgery was recommended only in extreme cases, because it always left the patient partially paralyzed.

In 1951, during one of these brain surgeries, Dr. Cooper was just about to cut the nerve pathway when a small artery in his patient's brain ruptured. Dr. Cooper clamped the artery shut. This action, while necessary, was also likely to cause brain damage, since the clamp closed off the blood supply to part of the patient's brain. Intuitively, Dr. Cooper left the clamp in place and stopped the operation.

When his patient awoke from anesthesia, the symptoms of shaking palsy were gone—and there was no paralysis. Apparently, closing off that particular artery had destroyed the cells responsible for sending the involuntary messages to the patient's muscles. Hoping this discovery might lead to a cure for involuntary movement disorders, Dr. Cooper conducted experiments to validate his finding. He found that clamping an artery gave unpredictable results, so he devised a way to kill the targeted brain cells with drops of alcohol. He called this procedure chemothalamectomy.

Though Dr. Cooper was a gifted surgeon and chemothalamectomy was shown to eliminate involuntary movements associated with various neurological disorders, including cerebral palsy, an individual brain sometimes responded the wrong way to the procedure and the patient's condition became worse. The negative publicity resulting from his surgical failures, his experiments on human subjects, and his own self-important behavior, fueled the controversy surrounding Dr. Cooper's work. None of this, however, seemed to staunch the flow of people with movement disorders who came to him for help.

Dr. Cooper first examined me at the NYU Medical Center in 1958. He was a very persuasive man and pressured my parents to allow him to operate on my brain. But upon further inquiry, my parents learned that I would be given only local anesthesia during the operation. They realized I would be fully conscious as Dr. Cooper drilled a hole in my skull, inserted a rubber tube deep into my brain, and probed in search of my damaged brain cells. I had to be alert so that Dr. Cooper could observe my reactions and thus locate the malfunctioning brain cells. Then, Dr. Cooper would send a few drops of alcohol down the tube and hopefully destroy the right cells. Mom and Dad refused to subject me to such a frightening and dangerous procedure. Dr. Cooper was confident of his ability to the point of being trigger-happy with his scalpel, yet my parents held firm. They would not risk losing the mental and physical abilities I had. They would wait and hope that someday someone would develop a better procedure.

If my parents had asked me to have brain surgery, I would have entered Dr. Cooper's operating theater without questioning their judgment. I was too young to weigh the risk against the possible gain. Later, I saw the results of the operation first-hand and came to appreciate the wisdom of their caution. In the mid-1960s, Mother's Aunt Sarah was diagnosed with Parkinson's disease and went to Dr. Cooper for a cryothalamectomy. Though she was an older woman and had other medical problems, the procedure relieved her tremors somewhat. But a cerebral palsied boy I met during my year at the A. Harry Moore School was not so fortunate. Before his cryothalamectomy, this boy was alert and able to walk. When I observed him some time afterwards he was sitting slumped in a wheelchair. He was unresponsive, his arms and legs were limp, and drool slithered down his chin. These results may show that cryothalamectomy was best used to treat Parkinson's Disease, because it was obvious that this boy should not have let Dr. Cooper pick his brain. That may be a crude phrase to use, but from my perspective, it underscores how serious the consequences of brain surgery can be.

Dad continued to follow the outcome of Dr. Cooper's experiments and sometime during my first year at the University of North Dakota, told me about Dr. Cooper's latest development: an electrical brain stimulator. The idea behind the stimulator was to relax muscle tension and spasticity by stimulating healthy brain cells to work overtime to compensate for damaged ones. This was accomplished by implanting two platinum electrodes on the base of the brain and two receivers under the skin on the patient's chest. The receivers, when connected by wires to a battery-operated transmitter, sent a constant electrical stimulus to the electrodes on the brain. The two-year-old technique had successfully controlled involuntary movement in a good number of otherwise untreatable patients. Dad felt satisfied that the risk associated with this procedure was fairly low. After I returned from Mark's wedding in California, Dad and I scheduled a preliminary examination, to at least see if I was a candidate for surgery. I was.

Dr. Cooper scheduled my brain stimulator surgery for the following summer. Meanwhile, it was hard to keep my hopes from rising too high. I kept wondering what my body would be like after the operation, and sometimes my imagination produced images of the miraculous. I was twenty-six years old and in the prime of my life. Though I refused to indulge myself in self-pity, I certainly felt the stinging reality that certain doors in life were closed to me because I was physically incapacitated. Unless something changed for the better, I knew that marriage, in particular, seemed unlikely for me. Consequently, I welcomed any improvement I might gain from the surgery, no matter how small it might be. During the year of waiting for the surgery, the same year I moved from the English department to the music school, my Christian friends encouraged me and prayed for me.

The home of Dr. Cooper's internationally known center for the treatment of involuntary movement disorders was St. Barnabas Hospital, located in the middle of a dirty, run-down section of the Bronx. Candidates for the brain stimulator stayed in the hospital for three weeks of testing and returned later for the actual procedure and an eight-week stay. I did not want to interrupt my schooling, so Dad arranged for my surgery to follow the preliminary testing without delay.

Preliminary testing was exhausting and frustrating. No matter how much I tried to cooperate, my body just wouldn't. The workers understood this and never showed irritation when my involuntary movements made their work difficult. The brain scan and EEG upset me the most because I had to lie perfectly still for a long time. Of course, this was impossible. Finally the technicians gave me a sedative and called in some men to hold my body as motionless as possible.

At this point in his career, Dr. Cooper traveled and lectured all over the world. His assistant, Dr. Ishmael Amin, handled the surgical preliminaries and monitored the recovery. We saw very little of the illustrious Dr. Cooper. Dr. Amin stressed to my father and me that any improvement from the brain stimulator would come about through a gradual learning process. We would not see overnight change. I knew Dr. Amin was being realistic, but it was hard for me not to imagine the possibility of gaining control over my muscles and maybe even walking someday.

Early Tuesday morning, June 24, 1975, they shaved my head. Sooner than I expected, I was wheeled into the operating room. I was nervous, but confident that no matter what happened to me, Jesus Christ was in control of my life. The last thing I remember thinking before the anesthesiologist put me to sleep was: Lord Jesus, let Your will be done . . .

Recovering from the operation was a nightmare. I thrashed, fighting the tube sticking down my throat, the oxygen mask on my face, and a terrific headache. I only wanted to rest undisturbed, but the people in the recovery room wouldn't let me. They were constantly moving me and checking something. They gave me a shot to ease the pain and later I was moved to a private room and kept under constant watch for 24 hours. Dad was with me. It was the sixteenth anniversary of Mother's death.

That evening, my brain began to hemorrhage. Barely conscious, I had no idea what was happening to me. All I knew was that I could not relax. I was very tired and very thirsty. Dr. Amin was alerted and returned to the hospital. Dad came racing back from home. I realized something was wrong when Dr. Amin ordered x-rays and blood tests. I started to panic, but his encouraging look reassured me. Really, he was very concerned about me. I was taken back to surgery, and Dr. Amin re-opened the incision, flushed out the blood clot that had formed between my skull and brain, and stopped the bleeding. Later, when I was resting comfortably, Dr. Amin said, "When we called your father to come back, his hair turned from gray to white in one hour!"

Two weeks later, Dr. Amin connected the wires leading from the battery-operated transmitter to the receivers in my chest. He switched on the brain stimulator. An electrical impulse surged through my brain. The dramatic change I half expected . . . did not happen. Now I looked like Frankenstein's monster and I had a headache that made me feel like him, too. During the eight weeks following the operation, Dr. Amin experimented with the strength of the electrical impulse, trying to find the voltage and rate that were best for me. Once my hair grew back I looked better, but the pounding headache, a side effect of the stimulator, required continuous strong medication. Fortunately, the discomforts only lasted about six months or a year. Beside the medication I took to ease those terrible headaches, I took my usual medication to control involuntary movements. Month by month I reduced the amount of medication I took. Gradually I felt more alert. Headaches ceased to be a big problem and my involuntary movements diminished. Thankfully, electrodes on the brain did not diminish my mental process or personality.

Measured over time, I would say the brain stimulator was of more value to me than all the years I spent in rehabilitation centers. The stimulator overrides my damaged brain cells to such an extent that when I turn it off for just a couple of hours, my involuntary movements become forceful, my speech becomes almost impossible to understand, and I get a terrific headache.

When I returned to North Dakota in September of 1975, Dave Stocker and I tried to put together enough courses to amount to a degree in operatic music literature. Unfortunately, the course selection at the University of North Dakota was limited. The task was nearly impossible, so at Dave's suggestion, I started looking for a school with a bigger music department. A series of interviews and inquiries I went though at the Vocational Rehabilitation Office pointed to Indiana University. Indiana's School of Music sounded like the perfect place to study opera—the catalog described a complete opera theater on campus. The thought of transferring to Indiana frightened me a little. North Dakota had been my second home for seven years. It would be very hard to leave my Christian friends and start over. But my calling was irresistible.

Dave arranged to fly with me to Bloomington, Indiana, in October. He not only wanted to help me through the interview process, but also wanted to see what difficulties my wheelchair would encounter on the Indiana campus. The concern Dave showed for me, a handicapped student, was a rare blessing. It was the work of God that this man came into my life at just the right time.

The day Dave and I flew to Indiana, our plane rose above the flat, snowy North Dakota horizon and turned south. Hours later we were in the hilly Hoosier heartland, soaking up fall colors and the warmth of an Indian summer day. The change in climate alone was enough to convince me that I should transfer to Indiana right away! Interviews at the Admissions Office and School of Music went well, but the handicapped facilities on campus were a disappointment. The university didn't even have a separate department of handicapped services. My main concern, naturally, was finding men who could assist me physically. The Admissions Office promised to locate a roommate for me, but I knew from experience that it wouldn't be easy.

My plans were almost complete when I sprang the news on Dad and Charlotte. They were surprised because I had said little to prepare them, but they were pleased. Though I depended on my parents financially, they prodded me to take initiative and to go after the things in life that were important to me. "If you fail, no big deal," Dad would say. "You can always pick up where you left off. The only failure you need to be ashamed of is the failure to give something your best shot."

During my last weeks in North Dakota, my emotions were mixed. I wanted to study opera, but I dreaded starting all over again at a new school. If the Admissions Office found a roommate for me, I'd probably end up with the same type of guy who had roomed with me at the beginning of my college career. To be on the safe side, I sent a notice to the Navigators and to Emmanuel Baptist Church in Bloomington saying that a handicapped student transferring to Indiana University needed a roommate. Then I decided to stop worrying. If God wanted me in Indiana, He would provide the man.

Six weeks later Dave Stocker received a phone call from the I.U. Admissions Office. They did not have anyone to room with me for the spring semester beginning in January 1976, and suggested that I apply again in August. No roommate in Indiana! This was hard for me to accept, especially since I had not heard from either the Navigators or the church in Bloomington. But it was already early December 1975, and it was unlikely that anyone would respond to my notice this close to Christmas vacation. I tried not to be discouraged and reluctantly made arrangements to spend the spring semester in Grand Forks.

Some days after I had resigned myself to my fate, I was listening (as I usually did each morning) to a portion of the Living Bible on cassette tape. The telephone interrupted. "This is Rick Beets," the voice on the line said. "I'm a student at Indiana University and I heard about you from some guys at the Navigator fellowship. Are you still looking for a roommate? Because if you are, I'm interested."

That phone call was a clear instance of divine intervention. An answer to prayer. A miracle. The boldness of my faith increased as a result. This boldness, however, was not a presumption that God would give me whatever I asked Him for. No, this was an assurance that God would supply my needs according to His Will. And because I went to Indiana University fully convinced that God knew what was best for me, I was able to emerge from the coming trials with my faith intact.

In early January, Dad and I flew from Newark to Indianapolis and drove a rented car south from there to Bloomington. It was cold and gray outside as we drove into town. The spring semester was at hand, and I was excited and sure of myself. Dad, usually a wise-cracker, was quiet. "Don't worry, Dad," I said. "Everything will be all right."

He forced a smile. "I sure hope you're right."

We were resting in our motel room when Rick called. He was already at the dorm, waiting for us to arrive. Everything I needed to get settled at the university fell smoothly into place. By the time he headed north, alone in the rented car, Dad's anxiety for me was at rest.

CHAPTER 10

My Indiana Home

At the University of North Dakota I had been one of 8,600 students. At Indiana University, I was one of 32,600! This population explosion might have overwhelmed a Dakota farm boy, but to a New Yorker like me it was nothing.

I was, however, a little disappointed with Indiana's campus. There were many physical barriers for handicapped students. I tried to keep in mind that I had chosen Indiana for its excellent School of Music, not for its facilities, but there were times when my frustration got the best of me. The university was aware of its problems and tried very hard to accommodate me. For instance, when I discovered that my wheelchair was too wide to pass through the bathroom door in my dormitory room, the maintenance crew remodeled the doorway. And since I couldn't use the steps leading to the main entrance of my dormitory, I was given a key to the service elevator in the back. From there, to get to my room, I had to pass through the cafeteria, which was usually locked. Because I carried so many keys and always came and went through the back door, I felt like a janitor. Still, those were minor inconveniences compared to finding the elevator out-of-order in the music building. When that happened, I had no choice but to miss class. Those occasions were exasperating, but common to all wheelchair users on campus. The fact is, my worst difficulties at the university came from my relationships with other people.

I had, more than once during my academic career, to adapt to a difficult instructor. I suppose the worst was that female Elizabethan drama instructor I had clashed with in North Dakota. The ghost of that woman haunted me in one of the first classes I took during the spring of 1976, a course on the literature of music. I handed in my first test thinking I had done fairly well. My paper came back to me a few days later with a low grade. After class I tried asking the professor to show me what I had done wrong, but she avoided making eye contact with me and pretended I didn't exist.

I reported the incident to my advisor. He claimed to know this instructor and said, "Oh, she's like that with everybody." When that answer didn't seem to satisfy me, my advisor dismissed the instructor's behavior by telling me he thought she had emotional problems. It seemed to me that if the woman's problems were that overwhelming, she had no business teaching a class. She was one of the most arrogant professors I have ever encountered. Later I found out that she was not a professor at all. She was a graduate student teaching an undergraduate course, a common practice at Indiana.

I must repeat, however, that for every difficulty I encountered, the university was more than willing to accommodate my needs. They classified my major as independent learning and whenever I needed help, provided student instructors to tutor me. When I caught on to the way things worked at the university, my grades improved.

I found my professors (the real ones) to be very understanding of my needs. My music theory professor, for example, made a special effort to ask me whether or not I understood the material. Eventually, my advisor found Margaret Strong, a piano instructor, who helped me on a regular basis. Margaret coached me through the technical and theoretical music courses and taught me how the elements of music make a piece sad, joyful, or dramatic. Thanks to her, though I did not have the advantage of playing an instrument, I was able to pass these difficult courses.

Considering what else went on in my life during the spring semester, it seems amazing that I did well at all. Early on, several Christians invited me to attend a Bible study in the dorm lounge. I was amazed to learn that many Christian men lived in the building. I also learned how naive I was about the different types of people who call themselves Christian. During one Bible lesson, someone told me I was not really a Christian because I had never been healed of cerebral palsy. Others in the group agreed: something was lacking in my faith.

I'd never heard such nonsense! "It is up to God to change a person," I said, but my words were barely understandable. God had changed me quite a bit, but I couldn't communicate to these guys even a part of what I'd been through. They couldn't hear over my speech difficulty and they couldn't see beyond my wheelchair. Their hypocrisy disgusted me, so I stopped going to Bible studies in the dorm. They continued to believe I wasn't a Christian because I couldn't walk.

To complicate my life further, early in the spring of 1976, at a recital at the music school, I met a young, talented singer from Puerto Rico named Maria. She loved the same music I loved and she was also a Christian. Our paths crossed with increasing frequency, and soon Maria was coming to visit me in the dorm. Sometimes I invited her to have a meal with me in the cafeteria. Instead of asking my roommate to come along, she helped me through the line and fed me.

I owned a car, but of course, others drove it for me. Maria could pull me out of my wheelchair and put me in the front passenger seat. We went to concerts, operas, and the Navigator and Campus Crusade for Christ meetings together. I even talked her into taking a class with me. She was required to take the class anyway, but scheduling it with me just gave us another excuse to be together. We really didn't need to invent reasons for being together. Maria and I were falling in love. For the first time in my life, I felt loved by a woman who saw me for what I was—a complete person: a man.

My physical handicap was not an obstacle to our relationship until Maria's father came to visit her. After she introduced us, he deliberately turned his body away from me and spoke very loudly to someone else. He obviously couldn't stand to look at me. When I told Maria how insulted

I felt, she tried to smooth over her father's behavior. This incident was my introduction to Maria's conflict between her loyalty to her family and her affection for me. I didn't understand it at first, but I eventually realized she was torn and confused the way Lulubelle, my old dog, had been when Gerald had called from one direction and Dad had called from the other.

One of the first friends I made when I moved into the dormitory was Barry Stevens. Throughout the school year, Barry showed himself to be very kindhearted, often going out of his way to help me. He was one of the few people I have ever encountered who did not see me as a handicapped person, but rather as a person who just happened to have a physical disability. I went with him to visit his family in Ohio, and later, he came home with me to visit my family in New Jersey. While we were in New Jersey, Maria, Barry, and I attended Maria's brother's graduation. After the ceremony, Maria's brother invited us to his apartment along with Maria's mother and younger sister. The tension in the room was very high because of the prejudice they had against my handicap. I should have paid more attention to the difference between Barry's response to my disability and Maria's, but I ignored the warnings.

After his graduation, Barry moved to New York City. I was involved with Maria and busy with school, but Barry and I kept in touch with an occasional letter or phone call and visit when I was in the New York area. Barry's last letter to me was years later, and he indicated that he wanted to visit me soon. The date for the visit was not definite, but I expected him to call any day to arrange things. Two weeks after I received Barry's letter, I got a call from my pastor at the time, Dave Brown. He wanted to tell me something, but not over the telephone. Dave came over to my house and sat down in my room in a chair beside me. "Barry Stevens' father just called me," he said. "Yesterday, Barry shut himself in a garage and took his own life."

At first, I was too stunned to think straight. "If only I had called Barry," I finally said. "Maybe I could have prevented this from happening."

Dave assured me it was not likely. "There must be more leading up to it than we know, Bob. More than Barry let on. All Barry's father told me was that Barry had been feeling lonely and confused about life."

I could only suppose that depression had motivated Barry's last letter to me. If that was the truth, it was cruelly ironic. Barry always had been the one who reached out to help others in need, but, when Barry had needed help for himself, he failed to reach out to others.

Dave tried to comfort me, but the consolation he offered was not equal to the hurt and sense of loss I felt. I had no doubt that Barry's soul was God's possession, but to this day, though I have never learned exactly what motivated Barry's suicide, I do not believe he made the right choice. We all face difficulties in life, but it is my firm belief that God is in control of every circumstance, no matter how difficult it might be for us to understand His purpose.

As for Maria and I, many of our friends were encouraging us to marry. Dad and Charlotte also observed our affection and kept hoping something would come of the relationship. But when Maria and I discussed the subject, she reminded me that an announcement would displease her family. Although I knew Maria's family didn't want her to get mixed up with me and I knew they hated my wheelchair and my mentally retarded-looking appearance, I felt strongly that as an adult, Maria should make her own choice. I wanted to force the decision; she wanted to avoid it. I thought her primary concern was securing her family's blessing on our marriage.

I didn't begin to face how deep the trouble ran until one of the Christian guys from the dorm (who later became my roommate) invited me to ride with him down to Louisville one day. The night before we left, I learned Ron's real reason for inviting me. He had arranged a private audience with the leader of a charismatic church. Ron had convinced himself that this man was going to heal me of cerebral palsy. At first, I refused to have any part of it. I knew God could heal me anytime He wanted to and was content to leave that decision up to Him. Ron pleaded; I was dumb enough to give in. To top it off, Maria rode to Louisville with us.

The charismatic leader was a bald man with a soft voice and a southern accent. To me, he seemed like an unsophisticated country preacher. Ron and Maria watched him anoint me with oil. Then the three of them placed their hands on my head and shoulders. The leader commanded Ron and Maria to start praying and while they prayed, he loudly rattled prayers of his own. I don't know what they expected to happen, but my crippled body continued to sit slumped in the wheelchair. They stood in awkward silence. I was silent, too, but I was also glad. This proved my point that God would change my life His way. Finally the leader dismissed us. "Wait a couple of days," he said. "See what happens."

Maria felt more confused than ever. Now she was pulled in a third direction: she wanted to believe I could be healed. "I just know God is going to work a miracle and heal you," she said. "Then we can get married." I certainly believed that God could work miracles—he had worked a miracle by just bringing me to Indiana—but I didn't believe I needed a miracle to get married. Nothing I could say persuaded Maria. It took me two and a half years to comprehend that she didn't want me as I was, only as she wanted me to become.

Self-doubt was Maria's disability. She seemed to depend on me for advice about everything, yet didn't seem to listen if I urged her in one direction or another. When she finally did make up her mind, she looked for visible signs, miracles, or emotional feelings to confirm whether or not she was acting according to God's will. This lack of self-confidence and lack of trust in the invisible work of God began to irritate me.

We both realized it was useless to continue the relationship and painfully parted, remaining friends. Maria moved to Chicago and continued studying vocal performance.

The move was overdue anyway. I had kept her at Indiana University longer than she ever had intended to stay.

I hurt deeply because Maria wouldn't marry me. Emotionally, I could not let go of her. My friends now suggested she was not the right girl for me, but nothing diminished my hope of being married to Maria some day. I had seen physically handicapped people marry and live normal lives. My mathematics teacher at the Crippled Children's School was such a man. He was in a wheelchair, but with his feet, this teacher could thread and operate a reel—to-reel tape recorder. He was married to a non-handicapped woman and had fathered a son. I admired him greatly.

I felt sure that Maria would change her mind about marrying me. In my judgment, her family was responsible for her preoccupation with divine healing. I furiously resented their prejudice against me. For a long, long time, I found it difficult to talk about Maria without in the next breath maligning her family. It was only by the grace of God that I gradually let go of the cancerous bitterness I felt towards them. The day I finally made the decision to forgive Maria's family was the day God healed me of an infirmity far more debilitating than cerebral palsy: hatred.

After that, I began to see that I had brought some of the problems on myself and on Maria by trying to force her to make decisions she really did not have the self-confidence to make. Because she had seen both her father and brother divorce their wives, I believe she harbored a deep fear of repudiation. In her mind, a challenge to her father's dictates might prompt him to disown her.

To this day, Maria has never married and has never done anything professionally with her beautiful singing voice. I think she gave up on both objectives too easily. My father believes she could have been a great vocalist if she had pushed herself more. That may be true, but then, she didn't have anyone like Mom, Dad, or Charlotte to push her until she learned to push herself. For some people, that's what it takes to succeed. Maria finally settled in Florida and became successful in the real estate business. Sometimes, when I'm making my annual drive from Indiana to Dad's Florida home, I plan a side-trip and pay her a visit. She still won't marry me, but I understand her better now, and our friendship has deepened through the years. Though it's not a storybook ending for a romance, it's a relatively happy one.

While I attended college, the responsibility for my care fell to a succession of hired roommates. Some of those men, such as Harold in North Dakota and Rick Beets in Indiana, were good friends as well as helpers, but I usually took whomever I could get. At Indiana University, the roommate who replaced Rick Beets claimed to be a Christian, but as I got know him better, I began to wonder if he was simply patronizing me. I discovered that he really didn't want to be in school; I don't know why he was there at all. He hung around our dorm room looking for opportunities to avoid schoolwork, and gradually I began to see that he was taking advantage of the fact that he had a handicapped roommate. He treated me like a child and tried to do too much for me. One morning, as he was preparing to get me out of bed and take me to the bathroom, I started to help myself up. (Even though I'm quadriplegic, I'm not paralyzed.) When this guy saw me struggling toward the edge of the bed, he became angry. He grabbed me and threw me backward, hard. It all happened very fast. My face hit the bedpost, stunning me physically and emotionally. Blood streamed from my nose. I held my breath, afraid that my least movement would infuriate him more. He seemed to calm down. Then he cleaned me up and dressed me. He put me in my wheelchair and left me alone in the room, where I sat, numb, for the rest of the morning. Both my Dad and Rick Beets had a talk with the guy and he never did anything like that again.

That incident should have taught me to be more selective about the men I chose to live with, but it took a few more bad experiences before I really learned my lesson. Ron, the guy who had taken me to the faith healer in Louisville, was actually a well-meaning, amiable fellow, so I eventually asked him to be my roommate. He enjoyed opera, but not quite as much as I did, so at first I paid no attention if he left the room when I played a tape or a stack of records. The problem was that Ron would disappear for hours. This naturally led to occasions when I had to use the bathroom before he returned. In such instances, I would knock the telephone receiver off the hook and use my left pinky to dial a friend's number before I became too desperate. Leaning over the desk, I spoke into the receiver and hoped the person on the other end wouldn't think it was a crank call and hang up. Sometimes I couldn't reach any of my friends by phone and my only hope was to get the attention of someone who might be hanging around the dorm near my room. Most of the guys I asked didn't mind helping me out once in a while, but Ron's continual dereliction of duty pushed some of my friendships to the breaking point.

Sometime after Maria moved to Chicago, I realized I was tired of dormitory food and dormitory life. Worse, I realized I was becoming a fixed component, not just in the dorm, but in the Navigator and Campus Crusade for Christ meetings. These gatherings attracted a young crowd, but now I was approaching thirty years old. I felt like an oddball and stopped going. I continued attending the Sunday morning worship service at a local church with my Navigator and Campus Crusade friends, but noticed, as I never had before, that the congregation was a composite of separate herds of college kids, married couples, and people in their 70s. I didn't fit in with any of those groups. I suppose that after my parting with Maria I started going through a mid-life crisis. I felt too old to be a student, too old to be a single, and too young to be an old man.

Harry Metzger, a young man who had been especially helpful to me during the semester when Ron had been my roommate, understood my awkwardness and invited me to try the small church he attended. I kept putting him off, because I had already met his pastor, Dave Brown, at a Bible study in Harry's room. Something Dave had said sounded different from my Baptist beliefs, and after my experience with the charismatics, I didn't want to get involved with a group where my theology didn't fit in. Harry didn't give up on me, and finally I let him take me to his church. As we entered the building that Sunday morning, people responded to Harry and me with warmth and love. The worship service was similar to the services I had been attending, and Dave's sermon turned out to be very down-to-earth. I couldn't find anything to complain about, so I went back to United Presbyterian Church many times, and Dave Brown became one of my best friends. He went out of his way to introduce me to the families in the congregation.

I was eager to become involved again in some kind of campus fellowship and Bible study group. I found what I was looking for when Dave Brunell, a friend from the music school, invited me to a Christian fellowship of American and international students sponsored by International Students, Incorporated. At those meetings, I found mostly older graduate students, men and women who were either approaching or who were already in their thirties. Many of them were somehow connected with the School of Music and shared my musical interests. I found out that one guy, David Canfield, collected classical music recordings. Many people I knew owned a few records, but in all of my years of collecting recordings, I'd never met another serious collector. David was a rare find in many respects. Besides being a composer, a cat lover, and a generous soul, he had the most obnoxious gift for spontaneous punning I have ever encountered. My new church and this group of students were just the tonic I needed to help me put my mid-life crisis behind me and get on with my life.

It's a good thing, too. It was now October of 1977, and my academic career was quickly drawing to a close. When graduation day finally came I was not in attendance. I still had not finished my final project, an independent study of two Verdi operas, and I assumed that I couldn't join my class in wearing a cap and gown. A few weeks after the ceremony had taken place, someone pointed out to me that it was possible to participate in the graduation with incomplete work. I would have received the recognition, but an empty diploma case.

I suppose I should have been disappointed after having worked so hard for so long, but I was not. As much as I loved Indiana University, the pomp and circumstance for its thousands of graduating students did not mark a great beginning for me as had the simple, Christ-centered commencement ceremony at the Crippled Children's School nine years earlier. I knew that my family wanted me to become "an official graduate," but I also knew that Dad found such ceremonies dull. I completed the requirements for my baccalaureate degree in August, 1979.

Three months later, Dad called to announce, "Guess what came in the mail today! Your diploma! It's now official—you're a college graduate!" I felt, as do quite a few graduates, like that diploma was a certificate of liberation. Having been a student for twenty-seven of my thirty-one years, I was eager to break free from academic life and taste the real world. I quickly discovered, however, that "life on the outside" was not going to be easy.

CHAPTER 11

Life on the Outside

I realized, months before graduating, that I needed to have a plan for life after school. For the first time in my life, my focus and attention would not revolve around school and a schedule. Dad needed plenty of advance notice in order to make arrangements for me if I moved back to New Jersey. I had always called New Jersey "home," but the truth was, I no longer felt at home there. I knew I was loved, but the extent of my family's conversation with me was, "Bobby, how are you doing?" or "Bobby, what's new?" It was shallow stuff, but after all, my relatives had seen me only a few times a year for the past thirteen or fourteen years. It's no wonder they still thought of me as the kid they remembered. That it bothered me was another problem I associated with my mid-life crisis. Anyway, I didn't think there was much in New Jersey to attract me beyond the love of my immediate family, Auntie Ann's baked goodies, and, of course, the Metropolitan Opera.

I felt more at home in Bloomington. God's grace had brought me here. I thought maybe that I should rent an apartment, as Charlotte had suggested some time ago. The more I prayed about the possibility, the more I found myself praying, not for an apartment, but for a house. At first the idea seemed unrealistic, but the more I thought about it, the more I thought, "Why couldn't God find a way for me to live in a house? Didn't He work the miracle that brought me to Bloomington in the first place?"

When I called Dave Brown and told him about my crazy idea, he didn't think it was crazy at all. Later, he came to my room in the dorm for a brainstorming session and filled a page with notes. I needed a house with one story, space to build a wheelchair ramp at the entrance, hallways wide enough for a wheelchair, enough bedrooms for myself and at least three other men, and a good location close to the university campus.

A few days later Dave made an appointment for me to meet Peggy Watson, a local Realtor. Peggy attended Dave's church but had never spoken to me. Like some people, she held back because she was afraid she wouldn't be able to understand what I said. I found out later that she even felt uncomfortable taking me as a client. Not knowing any of this, I was excited as I went to the church office to meet Peggy. I was even more excited when she said, "There's a house matching everything on your list just down the street from the church. We could look at it today."

Peggy was embarrassed when she had to ask me to repeat words she didn't understand. Everybody is that way at first. But as we looked at the house, she got over her fear and we conversed very naturally.

The house near the church had an unusual design feature. The main entrance was not on the front of the house, but on the side, sheltered under the carport. It was the perfect place to build a wheelchair ramp. The house had three bedrooms, one wide hallway, and everything was on one level. Peggy showed me other houses, but no other house for sale in Bloomington compared to the first house we looked at. I told Peggy it was an answer to prayer, another miracle. She agreed.

When I told Dad I wanted to buy a house, he thought I was crazy, but came to Bloomington to see the situation for himself. Right away Dad's keen business sense told him that buying a house close to the campus would be a good investment. As we talked through my plan, he agreed that having four roommates share the responsibility of taking care of me would make an ideal situation. The tricky part would be finding the roommates. The way I envisioned it, four or five capable guys would work for me in exchange for low cost room and board. This would not only help me, it would allow me to help financially struggling men. My home would be my ministry. Dad and Gerald arranged the financing and the house was mine.

The dormitory was closing for the summer, so Peggy arranged for my roommate and I to stay in a motel until the house was ready. There was one problem: this roommate was a guy who tried to do too many things at once. He had also taken a summer job as a painter and started work the morning after we moved into the motel. Dave Brown had planned to have breakfast with me at a restaurant that same morning and fortunately, I had asked him to come early and help me get ready. He was very concerned about the set-up at the motel, and so was I. Apparently my roommate envisioned me lying in bed all day while he painted houses. It wasn't going to work. I began going over my options when Dave said, "Bob, why don't you just stay with Marsha and me until your house is ready?" I thought that might be asking too much, but Marsha agreed with Dave. I would be better off staying at their house.

The next day my roommate and I checked out of the motel and into the Browns' home. Other families from the church donated food to help them feed the extra mouths, but Dave refused to accept any payment from me. Dave and Marsha's children included me in their games and made me feel right at home. After years of living with adults and with college-age men, it was fun to stay with a happy Christian family like the Browns. I felt even happier to be out of the dorm forever. While I stayed with the Browns, I was busy getting my house ready for occupancy. Friends from church and the university were enthusiastic about the project. They volunteered to paint, hang pictures, make curtains, build the wheelchair ramp, and make minor repairs. I bought a few pieces of furniture and new wall-to-wall carpet—a stylish avocado green shag. Three of my friends, including Dave Brunell, volunteered to be my first housemates.

On May 14, 1979, one of my housemates pushed my wheelchair up the ramp and opened the front door. This was it. We were moving in. As the wheels of my chair bumped over the threshold and rolled softly across the new shag carpet, I prayed silently for wisdom to carry out the responsibility and ministry God had entrusted to me.

On Sunday afternoon, June 24, 1979, Dad and Charlotte, my friends from the university, and most of the members of the church congregation gathered at my home for the formal dedication of my house to God. Dave took his place in front of the crowd and said:

> "We ought to dedicate our homes and their usage to God, but the more significant dedication we make today is the dedication of the members of Bob's household.
>
> Bob, you have an opportunity and a responsibility to extend God's blessing to each man who rooms here. It won't always be easy, so take charge for our Lord's sake, that grace and peace may abound.
>
> "Take charge by regular sharing of the Word of God and by prayers for all who are under your care. Lead by your example of joyful fulfillment in Christ, even when all of your desires are not fulfilled.
>
> "May each man who lives here, and each person who visits, be led to identify with God's people through Jesus Christ our Lord."

I wanted my home to be a place where men could serve one another the way Jesus taught his disciples to serve one another. That was easy to say, but hard to do. Even mundane things like doing dishes and laundry caused resentment and arguments among my housemates. Since most disagreements centered on whether or not someone was carrying out his responsibilities, I gradually developed written guidelines describing the chores that needed to be done, the responsibilities each man had to me, and a few behavioral standards for us all to follow.

As time went on, I began asking each new member of my household to agree in writing to follow Jesus' Matthew 18 instructions whenever problems came up. By this rule, we do not talk behind each other's backs or hold grudges, but go directly to the individual who is causing the trouble and talk things out. Only when private discussion won't resolve the difficulty do we ask others to get involved. Making the Matthew 18 procedure clear from the beginning got to the root of the problem and went a long way toward keeping a warm, relaxed atmosphere in my home.

I refer to the men who live with me as my helpers and brothers in Christ. God provides them in answer to prayer. Almost every one of them has been a blessing, both to me and to the other men who have shared my home. Only a few men have seemed to be a curse, and so stubborn that it was necessary to invite the elders of my church to hear the matter of disagreement. There were times, fortunately not many, when I thought it best to simply ask a man to move out. No matter what the circumstance, though, Jesus' formula for living has never failed to help me maintain the spirit of harmony and respect among my housemates that is so important to me.

I don't know any other adult as severely physically handicapped as I am who lives the kind of "inter-dependent" life I live. Most, I'm sure, have no choice about what happens to them. They end up in nursing homes. It is the generosity of my family, of course, that financially helps to make my freedom possible. Their love and encouragement are precious gifts to me that have come from the hand of God. Dad and Gerald trust me to use my resources wisely, and I do — until I hear a video recording or a compact disc calling my name. Then I lose any of the Kaplowitz practicality that has rubbed off on me and reach for my credit card.

My passion for recordings began after Mother's death, when I took over her record collection. I played her records over and over until they became so scratched that I threw them away. The task of replacing the worn records became such an absorbing avocation for me that 40 years later,

Mom's assortment of about 120 LP records and album sets has expanded to thousands of LP, CD, and video recordings.

My housemates, many of whom know nothing about classical music or opera, find themselves learning quite a bit as they help me build and organize my collection. Once I went with a housemate into a music store in search of a certain compact disk recording. I asked my housemate, a native Hoosier, to find the recording that had an RCA label. But Steve Waye's mid-western ear failed to make proper sense of my "New Joysey" enunciation of "RCA." He searched through the CDs in the opera section twice before giving up. "Bob," he said. "They don't have anything with an Ostrich Egg label."

Not only do my housemates receive an education in classical music and opera, but they also get to accompany me on my many travels. I enjoy travel, and visit my family in New Jersey and Florida two or three times a year. The rest of my travel budget is devoted to jaunts to Cincinnati, Chicago, or cities where there is a concert or performance that catches my interest. One of my most cherished ambitions had been to attend performances in each of the famous, historic opera houses of Paris, London, Vienna, Italy, and Germany. After several summers of traveling through Europe, the dream became reality.

In all of my years as a handicapped traveler, I have never experienced in Europe a reaction like I got at New York's Lincoln Center when I burped involuntarily during a performance. The woman in the seat ahead of me jerked her face in my direction and snapped, "Why don't you just LEAVE!" Incidents like that are rare, but they do happen. People in Europe, as far as I can tell, are less likely to take exception to the handicapped. Unfortunately, thieves also grant us equal treatment, as I discovered the day some urchin of Venice made off with my cash, credit cards, traveler's checks, and airplane ticket.

Of the many times I've been to Europe, the summer of 1977 stands out in my memory for two reasons. First, it was my return to Denmark after an absence of five years. I spent the first few days in the home of my beloved Ingrid. There had been changes in her life—her husband was dead—but in many ways, she was the same. She still had her job teaching retarded children. Yet, despite her years of experience in caring for the disabled, Ingrid failed to recognize that I had grown up. She tried to mother me again, and even told me to go lie down for a while during the afternoons. I knew she would have a fit if I refused, so instead of trying to tell her I was too old to be treated that way, I acceded to her wishes. After leaving Ingrid, I had a happy reunion with all my friends in Bjaert except Inger Kehlet, who had died the summer before.

The second reason I'll never forget that trip is Barry Stevens, the young man who accompanied me. Barry was one of the first friends I made at Indiana University when I arrived there in 1976. I've never met another person who enjoyed helping others the way Barry did. After he and I made the rounds in Denmark, we joined a tour group for the disabled in Germany and traveled through northern Europe. Barry was so considerate of everyone in the group that they took up a collection and presented him with this money as a surprise gift during the last meal we all had together.

Besides Denmark, my most frequently visited country in Europe is Italy. Italian art, especially opera, is a constant attraction. My first visit to Italy was in the late 80's as part of a study abroad program with Indiana University. I took a six-week course in art history over the summer, and I was hooked. I returned to Italy five or six times, the most recent visit during the summer of 2001. That summer was special. It was the centennial of the death of the great Italian opera composer, Giuseppe Verdi. I traveled that summer with Nathan Carter and Andy Halsey, two of my housemates.

We flew to Milan and rented a car. This was the beginning of our adventure, as no one knew how to drive a car with a manual transmission. After many starts and stops, Andy finally got the hang of it. His next trick, however, was to leave the emergency break on between the airport and the hotel. A couple of Italian men pulled up beside us on the highway and motioned vigorously that our car was smoking. We finally got the message. Car troubles aside, we had a fantastic experience traveling all over Italy and enjoying good food and seeing great art.

One pleasant experience was a conversation that I had with a waitress in Italian. We were at a small restaurant in Parma, and Nathan and Andy couldn't figure out what I wanted to order. So, finally, I decided to speak directly to the waitress in Italian, and she understood me! As we were leaving, I said "Ciao Bella!" and she liked it very much. I had no trouble returning to that particular restaurant later that week.

Since that trip to Italy in 2001, my travels have remained in the USA. I still travel to New York, New Jersey and Florida regularly to see my family and to enjoy the Metropolitan Opera. Chicago and Cincinnati are closer, and I use them more often for weekend trips. Apart from simply being enjoyable, these short trips have become an important recruiting tool. I've discovered over the years that a weekend trip to Chicago or Cincinnati is an excellent way to introduce potential housemates to my physical care and way of life. By taking me on a trip, a potential housemate has a much better idea of what to expect. I usually spend Christmas at the home of one of my housemates, and this has taken me all across the country.

Travel aside, leaving Indiana University for the "real world" didn't turn out as I expected. I had no work to do and no daily schedule to follow and found myself drifting from day to day, doing nothing but adding records to my collection and watching TV. Before too many weeks went by, I decided that I was tired of allowing myself to turn into a mental vegetable. To get my brain back on track, I registered for an art history class at the university. After I completed that course, I took another class and after that another. Finally, I began working toward a Master of Arts in musicology. Although it had not been my objective in the beginning, graduate school and the pursuit of my scholarly interests has become my life's work. This was certainly not the future imagined for me years earlier by Dr. Greenspan, the doctor who could see no possibility for a brain-damaged boy like me other than being "kept" in a home for life.

There had always been possibilities for me in life, of course, but only people who knew to look beyond my wheelchair, my physical disability, and my youthful inexperience could see them. Nevertheless, the ability to recognize distant possibilities could not make even one of them become reality unless I supplied the ambition, determination, and responsibility to make the most of my opportunities. Like many young people, I didn't always show that I had what it took. Even Dr. Carlsen doubted that I would ever finish college. In the end, with the help of my loving family, I not only succeeded in my academic endeavor, but also faced and overcame many obstacles in life.

I discovered along the way that overcoming obstacles in life is a growth process requiring hard work, a practical strategy, and daily dependence upon God's grace. The process of growth is not always obvious, for it takes place in the mind. And there are seasons of change and seasons of rest. That's why it is important, especially when responding to a person who has a physical handicap, not to be misled or intimidated by an outward appearance.

Each of us has imperfections to acknowledge. Each of us has obstacles to overcome. And each of us has possibilities to grasp.

APPENDIX

Life on the Inside

by Lucas D. Weeks

Located just south of Indiana University's campus, Bob's house looks pretty normal from the outside. In fact, you might just miss it if you didn't know what to look for. A few telltale signs might include the handicapped stickers on the dark blue Dodge Grand Caravan parked in the driveway, and perhaps the wooden ramp that extends from the edge of the carport to the front door. After living in the community for nearly thirty years, Bob's house is boringly normal to the locals.

If you are fortunate enough to find yourself making your way up the ramp and through the front door, however, you will begin to realize that Bob's house is anything but "boringly normal". Standing at the front door, you would see a piano on your left, some couches and chairs and a TV to your right, and the face of Giuseppe Verdi straight ahead, staring you down. Once you muster up the courage to pass by "mean Joe Green" and head down the hallway to the left, you would soon find Bob's room.

Upon entering, the first thing you notice is the stereo at the back of a desk that is in the center of the room. There are windows on either side of the desk, with a television sitting on a chest of drawers in front of the window on your left, and a bed beneath the window on your right. Just on the other side of the bed is a shelf that is full of opera DVD's. Every other inch of wall space directly opposite the door is covered with shelves. Books, magazines, and LP's line the shelves—and almost all of them are somehow related to opera. When you take a few steps into the room and turn around, you are greeted with the sight of more shelves covering every inch of wall space — only this time, the shelves are packed with compact discs. Thousands of them. While opera dominates the collection — Bob has over thirty versions of certain favorite operas — his musical collection also includes other types of classical music, jazz and Broadway musicals.

CD's and books aside, it is Bob and the men who live with him that make his house a very special place. Aside from Bob's room, there are now three bedrooms that provide space for a total of six "Bobbites". Men who live at Bob's house tend to stay anywhere from a single semester to a couple years. I've lived with him for five and a half years now, and, as far as I know, only one other Bobbite has lived with him that long.

To understand how truly amazing Bob and his house is, you need to understand that he is fully quadriplegic, and that he can only communicate with great difficulty. It is very challenging for those who are not trained by practice to understand his speech. His family lives roughly 800 miles away, and yet Bob has lived in his own home for 30 years. Bob needs help doing everything from taking a shower to getting up in the morning. By directing the men who live with him, he handles every major part of his own care without the direct involvement of either his family or a professional caregiver. How is this possible?

First, Bob is just so likable! Young men want to live with him, not only because of the monetary benefit that living with him offers, but also because he is so much fun to be around. No matter how embarrassing or awkward the situation, Bob is always ready with a joke and a smile.

But college guys are poor and hungry, and jokes won't fill one's stomach. In the early days, Bob enticed men to come and live with him and care for him by simply charging them next to nothing for rent. The close proximity to campus makes his home a prime location for IU students. That progressed into a policy of free room and board for all his Bobbites. With five or six men living in the house, each man would be required to spend roughly 18-22 hours per week "on shift" with Bob. Everything from going to class to shopping for food to getting Bob a drink of water in the middle of the night was covered. And all this by college men who had never had professional experience caring for the handicapped!

Over the years, Bob's care has gradually changed. Even within the time that I've lived with Bob, I've seen the amount of care that he needs gradually grow and become more intricate. When I first entered the house in January of 2003, for example, he was still able to put a very slight amount of weight on one foot. No longer. He has made two trips to the emergency room in the past two years, and the first trip was particularly serious. Over time it became clear to Bob and me that his house needed a little more structure. Bob will turn a venerable sixty years old this year, and his needs are simply not the same as those of a thirty year old. So we put our heads together this past year and implemented some very important changes to his care.

We began by tearing the house apart—literally. The house had needed some major renovations for years, and we decided that we might as well get to it. Old carpet was torn up and replaced with laminate. Bob purchased a new washer, dryer and dishwasher, and had the entire kitchen torn out and refinished. The old TV center and furniture in the living room was replaced. His room received a complete overhaul as well: new shelves, a new paint job, and, eventually, some new furniture. When the dust finally cleared, everyone agreed that Bobs house was much improved.

The most important change, however, is that there is now a "house manager" who is paid and answers directly to Bob and his family back in New Jersey. Ultimately, the house manager is there to ensure that Bob continually receives a very high standard of physical care. His list of responsibilities include creating the work schedule each semester, ensuring that the house itself is clean and well cared for, and ensuring that conflict within the house is resolved. David Canfield, Bob's longtime friend and fellow music lover, checks in on the house from time to time, and is available for consultation in the event of any serious problem or conflict. The other five Bobbites receive a stipend for their work, and answer to both Bob and the house manager. There is now a weekly house meeting in which the men talk about problems or concerns around the house, and plan for the coming weeks and months. A weekly cleaning schedule that is compulsory helps to keep the house clean and pleasant.

The system sounds great, but it only works if Bob can find dependable men to live with him. Bob has to personally recruit each man that lives with him, including the house manager. During the time that I've been here, most of Bob's new recruits have come from his current church, Church of the Good Shepherd. Aside from Indiana University's School of Music, Bob's church has been his main source of friendships and community life in Bloomington. Bob put his faith in Jesus back in 1970, and that faith is evident to this day. The men who live here may not be Christians, but they will all hear about, and experience in some measure, the love and mercy that is extended by God to them through Jesus Christ. And every man who comes into the house is exhorted to be patient with each other, to bear one another's burdens, and to love one another.

Though Bob's house is a very special place, it is by no means easy to live here. It is easy to forget that, considering Bob's condition in life, no one would have been surprised if he had ended up in an institution somewhere in the New Jersey area. That Bob has fought so long and so hard to stay out of institutions and to lead a full life is a testament to the support and encouragement of his family, and especially his father. But Bob's perseverance is not fully explained by his family's big-hearted support.

Indeed, Bob's evident faith is perhaps the most striking thing about him, and it permeates his home. It takes humility to allow someone else to care for you, particularly at your most vulnerable and private moments. Bob has depended on others his entire life, to be sure, but growing older will inevitably bring a new set of challenges. When Bob first moved to Bloomington, he was nearly the same age as those who cared for him. These days, Bob has to deal with the incongruity of being a 60-year-old man who is cared for by 20-year-old college sophomores.

And yet, once again, this is precisely where Bob's faith shines through. It would be easy for Bob to retreat to an institution where he wouldn't have to deal with the messy, day-to-day living that goes on in a house full of selfish bachelors. I have seen Bob approach men in his home and humbly ask them for forgiveness for getting angry with them. A 60-year-old man going to a punk 20-year-old kid—a kid who seemingly figured out how to wipe his own nose only yesterday—and asking him for forgiveness? Many 60-year-old men would rather die in an institution than face the indignity of living with young men where there would ever be a need to ask for forgiveness. And yet, Bob lives amidst this struggle, indignity and suffering with such aplomb that he's not only admirable—he's delightful. He is never bitter. When I ask him how he feels, he will often retort, with a big smile on his face, "How do you think I feel? I'm handicapped!"

In closing, Bob, allow me to speak to you from my heart and to give you a few exhortations directly. Do not grow weary in well doing! Faith never rests on its past laurels, but always presses forward into deeper communion with God. The temptation to find your rest and satisfaction and hope in your music and opera—to make a god out of this pleasure—will only grow stronger as you get older. You will be tempted to run from the humdrum of daily living and retreat into the solace of your own mind. Resist this temptation! Your home can be a place of service to others, and to the Church, for many years to come. Remember Jesus Christ, risen from the dead, the offspring of David. (2 Tim. 2:8) Remember that our Lord Jesus Christ suffered, and so we do not count it beneath us to suffer. Keep struggling! One day, your suffering will be over, and you will stand (yes, stand!) before God and worship Him.

But I do not account my life of any value nor as precious to myself, if only I may finish my course and the ministry that I received from the Lord Jesus, to testify to the gospel of the grace of God. (Acts 20:24)

Acknowledgments

Soon after I arrived in Indiana in 1976, Charlotte announced that she had started writing a book about me. When I told her that I'd rather write my own book, she presented me with the chapter she had completed, and said, "Here, you can take over." So I did. During the following eight years, working off and on, I typed over one hundred pages of narrative, intending that friends and family would read the finished product. The task was almost finished when one of my housemates, Tom Hoffman, encouraged me to think towards a larger audience. With publication as our goal, Tom began editing my manuscript. The project came to a standstill when he transferred from Indiana University to Covenant Seminary in St. Louis.

David Canfield and his wife Carole have been close friends of mine ever since David and I met at the Christian fellowship of American and international students in the late 1970s. At times, the Canfield home seems to be the crossroads of America. It was there, one afternoon in late August of 1993, while Tom Hoffman was visiting me from St. Louis, that Tom and I sat beside the pool wondering how I could finish turning my manuscript into a book. As Providence would have it, Isabel Hogue, another friend of the Canfield's and mine, joined the conversation. She agreed to take up the work where Tom had left off. Countless rewrites later, Isabel and I want to thank both Charlotte and Tom for getting the project started in the first place. We also want to thank Jason Harkness, Elizabeth Bortka, Dick Mawby, Yvonne Hanzal, Doris Nelson, Helen and Eric Rasmusen, Carole and David Canfield, and Sheryl and Brad Smith for their editorial advice and honesty.

I want to thank the Reverend David B. Brown, Jr. and Steven D. Waye for generously contributing their work to this volume, and to especially thank Ruth Bell Graham for granting permission for me to include her poem, "Odd this twisted form" from her book Sitting By My Laughing Fire.

I am indebted to my brother Gerald and his wife Nancy, who provided for the purchase of my house in Bloomington, Indiana; to their children, Tracy, Scott, Allison, and Cindy and their spouses; and of course, to my parents. Charlotte eventually divorced my father, for reasons that even now are not clear to my family. Dad has since married Joyce, a model of the same unselfish, comforting nature that characterized my mother Ruth.

I want to express my appreciation to the people of Grace Covenant Presbyterian Church and to its officers, Greg Brown, David Canfield, Jerry Hogue, David Wegener, and Bill Wood. Since the founding of the church ten years ago, the men, women, and children of the congregation have selflessly extended to me friendship and physical assistance for which I am deeply grateful. I am also grateful for the leadership and example of the Reverend John F. Peoples, who has encouraged me more than once through difficult circumstances.

Finally, I want to thank to all of the men who have been a part of my household, who have shouldered the responsibility of living in my domain. My only regret is that there isn't space here to name them all.

Bob Kaplowitz
August 1995

Acknowledgments for the Revised Edition

Unfortunately, Grace Covenant closed its doors in 1999. Since then, I've attended Church of the Good Shepherd, along with a number of my friends from Grace Covenant. David and Carole Canfield are still good friends, and I want to thank David for proofreading this revised edition of my book. Barbara Lehr, an English professor here at Indiana University, read through my first edition and gave me some very helpful pointers. I am grateful to Pastor Tim Bayly for providing the foreword, and to Lucas Weeks for giving his perspective as a "Bobbite".

Bob Kaplowitz
May 2008

Additional Reading
(Don't ignore your own mind.)

Cerebral Palsy

Geralis, Elaine, ed. CHILDREN WITH CEREBRAL PALSY: A PARENTS' GUIDE. 1991.

Hardy, James C. CEREBRAL PALSY. 1983. (A good historical background.)

Jewish Experience

Lowry, Lois. NUMBER THE STARS. 1989. (Historical fiction about Danish effort to shelter Jews from Nazis in 1943. For young readers.)

Biography

Brown, Christy. MY LEFT FOOT. London: Michelin House. 1954.

Carlsen, Anne H. (biographical sketch)

http://www.annecenter.org/about_us/annes_history.html

Cooper, Irving S. THE VITAL PROBE: MY LIFE AS A BRAIN SURGEON. 1981.

Martin, Carolyn. I CAN'T WALK SO I'LL LEARN TO DANCE. Zondervan. 1994.

Nolan, Christopher. UNDER THE EYE OF THE CLOCK. New York: St. Martin's Press. 1987.

Made in the USA
Monee, IL
14 January 2022

88969174R10083